July 1991.

To Maurice,

Congratulations on your

We hope the book brings back some happy memories.

Love from.

Nancy,

Ian & Family,

Arthur & Family &

Jan & Family.

THE ISLE OF MAN TT

AN ILLUSTRATED HISTORY 1907-80

MATTHEW FREUDENBERG

ASTON PUBLICATIONS

To Emily whose skateboard made
this book possible

Published in 1990 by Aston Publications Limited
Bourne End House, Harvest Hill,
Bourne End, Bucks, SL8 5JJ.

ISBN 0 946627 57 6

Designed by Chris Hand

Sole distributors to the UK
book trade,
Springfield Books Limited,
Norman Road, Denby Dale,
Huddersfield,
West Yorkshire, HD8 8TH.

Sole distributors for the USA,
Motorbooks International,
Osceola, Wisconsin 54020,
United States.

Printed in England by The Amadeus Press Limited,
Huddersfield.

Acknowledgements

For their advice and encouragement I am grateful to many individuals and organisations, among whom the following were particularly helpful; Brian Woolley of *The Classic Motorcycle*, for sharing his large personal knowledge of the subject, Kim White, motorcycle archivist at EMAP Publications, Nick Keig and Mary Evans of Keig Photographic, Isle of Man, Karl Reese and Dieter Herz for material relating to German TT participants, Colonel J. B. Mylchreest, Dennis Reed and Peter Kneale for patient help with photos on the Isle of Man, Debbie Clark at the Auto Cycle Union and the Manx Museum, Douglas. To Wendy, my wife, special thanks for typing and correcting manuscript, but above all, for her encouragement throughout the preparation of this book.

The excellent modern photographers who have provided pictures are acknowledged under their contributions. I must also mention the late John Greenwood, TT archivist extraordinary, not only for the comprehensive statistics that he has left to the sport (at the National Motor Museum, Beaulieu), but also for his boundless enthusiasm for the Isle of Man, shared with me in correspondence over several years. Any errors or omissions on the pages that follow are entirely my own.

Contents

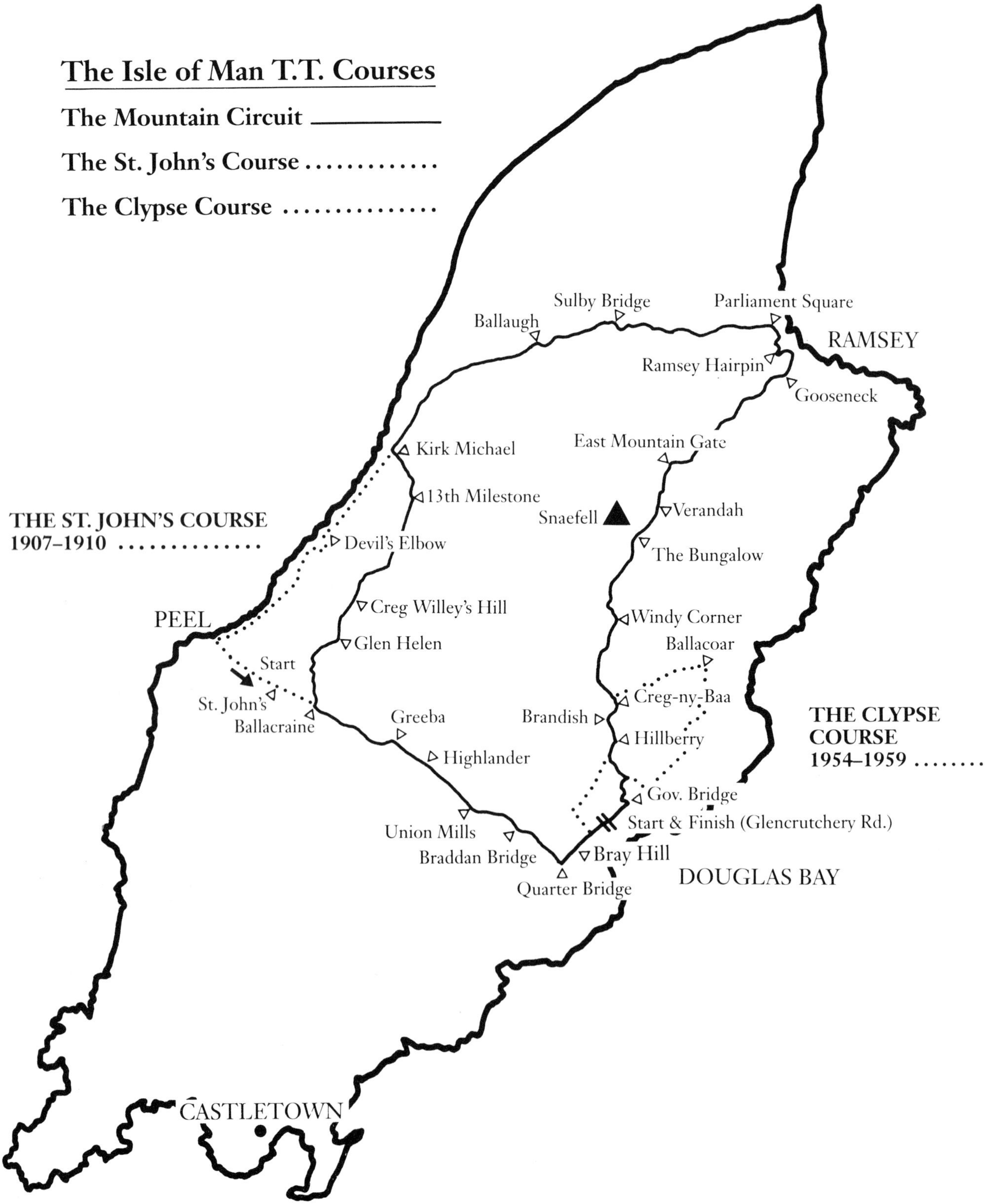
The Isle of Man T.T. Courses
The Mountain Circuit
The St. John's Course
The Clypse Course
THE ST. JOHN'S COURSE
1907–1910
THE CLYPSE COURSE
1954–1959
RAMSEY
PEEL
CASTLETOWN
DOUGLAS BAY
Sulby Bridge
Parliament Square
Ballaugh
Ramsey Hairpin
Gooseneck
East Mountain Gate
Kirk Michael
13th Milestone
Snaefell
Verandah
Devil's Elbow
The Bungalow
Creg Willey's Hill
Windy Corner
Glen Helen
Ballacoar
Start
St. John's
Ballacraine
Creg-ny-Baa
Greeba
Brandish
Hillberry
Highlander
Gov. Bridge
Start & Finish (Glencrutchery Rd.)
Union Mills
Braddan Bridge
Bray Hill
Quarter Bridge

INTRODUCTION

At the age of 14 I lapped the Isle of Man circuit in under ten minutes. This was not as impressive a performance as it sounds as I was straddling a school bench in Liverpool at the time, amazing my classmates with the swiftness of my downward changes as I followed Geoff Duke's line through Creg-ny-Baa. I was well infected by TT fever then, and although a motorcycle has replaced the school bench, the fever has not lost its hold.

Countless words have been written about the TT, the best of them by men who raced in them and had a gift with words as well – men like Geoff Davison, Graham Walker and Les Higgins. But there is still a place for an historical account of the race that has been the centre of motorcyclists' enthusiasm for more than 80 years, and I have tried to give life to the story with photographs that recall the atmosphere of the Isle of Man far better than words. The Tourist Trophy races have had great technical and commercial influence since the early days of motorcycling; they have produced great riders and inspired some fascinating machines.

In the 1950s almost all international motorcycle and car races took place on specially closed public roads, from Switzerland to Mexico, but some, like the Giro d'Italia, the Pan-American race and the Mille Miglia matched the TT for the beauty and danger of their course. Now, when flat and usually ugly autodromes have taken the place of the great road races, the TT is a unique and surprising survivor.

This history ends in 1980, the year of Joey Dunlop's first Classic TT win. The TT was entering a new phase: one of highly specialised TT riders, of a circus of motorcycling sideshows, and of endless controversy about safety.

This phase will have its own history in due time.

Overleaf:

***1:* BRAY HILL. *Immediately after the start comes the heart-stopping swoop down Bray Hill. Experienced riders accelerate all the way down and can exceed 150 mph at the bottom. Bill Ivy, here in 1966, hardly lifts his head as he travels flat out over a bump.* (EMAP) *2:* QUARTER BRIDGE. *A slow downhill corner at the southernmost point of the course. The lamppost has been removed since 1937, when this Keig shot of Freddie Frith was taken, but the corner is still a trap for the unwary.* (Keig) *3:* BRADDAN BRIDGE. *The sharp left and right swerves over Braddan Bridge require exact positioning of the machine. In 1923 the sidecar racers had many problems with this 'S' bend, Harry Langman finally crashing out of the sidecar TT while leading on the last lap, after clipping the kerb visible by the right-hand wall of the bridge.* (BBC Hulton Picture Library) *4:* BALLAUGH BRIDGE. *Leaping motorcycles at Ballaugh are a popular spectable, but most riders take this slowish hump very steadily. Helmut Fath makes a bit of a pig's breakfast in 1960, but it did not stop him from winning.* (EMAP) *5:* RAMSEY. *Kenny Howles charges through the town of Ramsey, two-thirds of the way round the 37 1/2-mile course. Having taken the slow right-hander his passenger poises to lean out for the faster left-hand exit from Parliament Square.* (Mike Corrin) *6:* RAMSEY HAIRPIN. *Frank Applebee, Scott, No 7, well lined up to pass a Triumph on the apex of Ramsey hairpin in 1912. The hairpin starts the climb to Snaefell, and in 1912 the Triumph rider would probably have to jump off and push up the steep bit after the bend, while Applebee's gearbox would allow him to drive up.* (EMAP) *7:* WATERWORKS. *Agostini changes gear between the series of fastish bends at the Waterworks, accelerating on up the climb to Snaefell.* (Mike Corrin) *8:* THE VERANDAH. *This fast section on the Mountain stretch was faster still after road improvements in the early 1970s. The road climbs on to the Bungalow, beyond the converging hills ahead. One of the wettest and most fog-bound sections of the course.* (EMAP) *9:* GOVERNOR'S BRIDGE. *First of two very slow bends as the course returns to Douglas, this awkward bend has caught out a few riders, including Stanley Woods, who is making a graceful job of it this time, while leading the 1936 Lightweight TT.* (Keig) *10:* PARKFIELD CORNER. *In pursuit of perfection on four wheels, Geoff Duke takes Parkfield Corner while leading the 1952 Empire Trophy Race in a works Aston Martin. This is the turning off the Glencrutchery Road which leads onto the Clypse Circuit, shortly after the start. Geoff had no luck with car racing in spite of showing great potential, and he returned to full-time motorcycle racing in 1953.* (Keig)**

1.

2.

3.

4.

5.

6.

7.

8.

9.

10.

Chapter 1:

Beginnings

> 'It was the 1906 International Race (in Austria) which led to the birth of the now famous Tourist Trophy Races . . .
> 'During the long train journey home, a discussion arose as to whether it would not be possible to promote a road race in England, where fair play would be assured' – *Charlie Collier – winner of the first TT.*

Fair play, it seems, was in short supply in the major International motorcycle competition of the 1900s, the International Cup Races. Held in France in 1904 and 1905, and in Austria in 1906, this event was contested by teams representing their own countries, and each time the host country's team was amply and illegally helped by local enthusiasts. In France it was tin tacks, scattered on the road in a pattern supposedly known to the French riders only; in Austria the Puch team were followed round the 39-mile course (lapped four times) by Puch sidecar outfits full of spare parts, tyres and mechanics, with shameless disregard for the race regulations. Puch were nevertheless declared winner of the 1906 cup in spite of a united protest from the other competitors. Charlie Collier took third place on a Matchless-JAP.

British motorcycles had made a poor showing in all three of the International Cup Races, mainly because of mechanical failures, and all this cheating was too much for Englishmen, who claimed that they played a straight bat. In fact it was too much for the other competitors as well, and after 1906 the race was no longer held.

So the idea of a British motorcycle race of international standing was promoted by prominent motorcyclists and committee members of the Auto Cycle Club in 1906. Among these were brothers Harold and Charlie Collier, their father H. H. Collier (founder of the Matchless Motor Cycle Company), H. W. Stavier and Etienne Boileau of *The Motor Cycle*. Also among them was the Marquis de Mouzilly St Mars.

The Marquis de St Mars was an active supporter of the British teams in the International Cup Races, helping with the problems of competing in foreign lands, and protesting on their behalf against their competitors' knavish tricks. It was probably he who persuaded the Auto Cycle Club to take on the organization of a race on the Isle of Man, to be called the 'Tourist Trophy Race'. It was certainly he who presented a magnificent trophy in the shape of Mercury, winged God of Speed, to the ACC for the future winners of the race.

An ACC committee, guided by Freddie Straight, worked out details of a course, regulations, costs and prize money. By the end of 1906 plans were complete and regulations were issued. The aim was to encourage development of roadworthy machines, so entries were required to have mudguards, silencers and toolkits; there was no place for the track-racing monsters with drilled frames and engines of up to two litres capacity that were fighting it out on the Continent. The winners of the single-cylinder and multi-cylinder classes were each to receive a trophy and prize money of £25. Second and third finishers in each class would take home £15 and £10 respectively.

The ever energetic Marquis de St Mars acted as one of the four judges of the race itself; no disgraceful foreign practices were going to mar Britain's first international road race, and the ACC set a date in May, 1907, for this historic event to take place.

In the early 1900s motorcyclists took over the banked cycle-racing tracks at White City and Canning Town for speed contests. Here a group of track racers relax with their machines. **(Manx Museum)**

The first and second International Cup races were held in France and were won by the French Griffon team. The French Champion, Lamberjack, demonstrates the winning style. **(EMAP)**

Before the start of the last International Cup race, at Patzau in Austria, Charlie Franklin stands by his factory Matchless of 6 hp (731cc). It has open exhaust ports, coil and accumulator ignition and rigid forks. Drilled pedal cranks helped to keep the weight below the regulation limit of 110 lb. Franklin failed to finish. (VMCC Archives)

Chapter 2:

The First TT Races 1907–10

THE FIRST TT, 28 MAY, 1907

> 'It was a queer-looking crowd on the village green. The grandstand, if my memory serves me, consisted of a couple of beer crates on which the officials stood' – *Laurie Cade*.

The circuit set out by Freddy Straight's committee was a rough triangle over on the west side of the Island, from St John's to Ballacraine, then along today's TT course via Ballig Bridge, Creg Willey's Hill and Barragarrow to Kirkmichael. There a sharp left took the course down the coast to Peel and back to St John's to give a lap length of 15 $^3/_4$ miles.

Although a mountain course had been used for car racing on the Isle of Man since 1904, the low power and fixed transmissions of motorcycles in 1907 made them incapable of tackling the slopes of Snaefell, up or down! The 'short' triangular course proved plenty tough enough, with a climb of Creg Willey's that needed either furious pedal assistance or a brisk push, with engine running and rider running alongside.

The regulations allowed unlimited engine size, but limited fuel consumption to 90 mpg for single-cylinder machines and 75 mpg for 'multis', which worried many competitors. Singles and multis raced for separate trophies, and 17 singles and eight twins rattled and chugged away in pairs from the start.

The race developed into a Matchless-Triumph battle (each firm entered two motorcycles), and countless stops for new plugs, belt repairs and punctures meant frequent changes of leader. After 4 hours 8 min and 8 sec Charlie Collier (Matchless) led Jack Marshall (Triumph) to the finish at St Johns. Rem Fowler (Norton-Peugeot) and Billy Wells (VINDEC) had similar troubles, and changes of lead, until Rem Fowler won the twin-cylinder class in 4 hours 21 min.

The fastest laps made by Collier and Fowler were 42.9 mph and 41.8 mph respectively.

Looking back 50 years later, Rem Fowler recalled making about ten stops for mechanical 'adjustments', including six plug changes, and repairs to a front tyre which burst at 55–60 mph, his top speed. He also remembered the frantic flag-waving of the Boy Scouts (to whom responsibility for marshalling the course was entrusted) when he rounded Devil's Elbow to find a machine in flames on the road in front of him. He missed it, and Fowler and the Boy Scouts served the TT for many more years.

1908

> 'Captain Arbuthnot arrived (for refuelling) in excellent spirits and said it was the biggest fun he had ever had in his life' – *The Motor Cycle*, 1908.

Burned fingers healed and weary leg muscles revived, most of the 1907 riders were back in 1908 in a much enlarged entry of 37 competitors, among whom were several foreign entrants. Regulations now banned pedals and imposed still stricter fuel limits of 100 mpg for singles and 80 mpg for multis.

A most elaborate system of fuel rationing allocated different-coloured petrol cans to riders of singles and multis, a blue can holding 1 gallon and a white can holding 4 pints 13 oz to singles and a green can holding 1 $^1/_4$ gallons and a can of a colour now forgotten holding 3 pints and 16 oz to multis. Pity the colour blind, and there were sad cases of cans being knocked over in the riders' haste to refuel.

As in 1907, Triumph fought Matchless. Jack Marshall was determined to win this time, but Charlie of the Collier brothers took the lead when Marshall fell off, and then broke a valve on the fourth lap. Amazingly, Marshall replaced the valve from the comprehensive collection of bits each rider carried with him, put his head down and gained steadily on Collier to win by 2 min 10 sec after 3 hours 54 min and 50 sec.

Harry Reed (DOT-Peugeot) won the multi-cylinder class from W. Bashall (BAT) and R. Clarke (four-cylinder shaft-drive FN.)

The IoM *Examiner* believed it had the explanation for Marshall's determination, 'A charming lady, so it was freely rumoured, had promised to make him a happy man, provided he was acclaimed first in his class.'

For 1909 fuel limitations were dropped and from now on single- and multi-cylinder machines competed directly in one race. The Matchless company profited from track experience to enter two 730 cc Matchless-JAP V-twins. Once again Jack Marshall made a charge from behind, but a broken valve ended his race as he was gaining on Harry Collier's Matchless and Lee Evans's Indian twin. This time his spare valve was the wrong size.

Collier galloped in to win at 49 mph, with a lap at 52.3 mph, with Lee Evans second by 40 sec. A. Sproston (Rex) rode into a ditch five minutes after the start, breaking his left ankle. He managed to restart but stopped at the end of the first lap to remove his boot. He then went on, pushing off with right foot only, stopped after lap 6 to refuel and continued to finish and win a well-deserved silver medal – an amazing bit of true grit.

The 15½ mile circuit was used for the last time in 1910 and by now the entry was 83 riders and machines. On a sunny May morning the 72 starters fit and present on race day set off in pairs for a race packed with incident, Matchless, Indian and Triumph fielding strong teams of experienced riders.

After the leading BAT ridden by H. H. Bowen ran into a wall and broke its frame, the Collier brothers took first and second places out of only 29 finishers. At Ballacraine a wooden banking was erected to allow riders a 'safer' passage through the bend. Nicknamed 'the Wall of Death', most riders gave it one try and thereafter avoided it, and Ballacraine remained the most popular bend for falling off.

Most of the machines that fell by the wayside simply broke down beyond repair, but others caught fire or left the road at speed. One man threw his motorcycle into a ditch in disgust; W. O. Bentley, later the famous car manufacturer, felled a policeman when the front tyre of his Indian punctured, but the most serious accident was in practice, when Alan Moorehouse crushed a leg so badly that it had to be amputated. Charlie Collier's winning speed was 50.63 mph, still with direct belt drive from crankshaft to rear wheel. The winning machine was low slung and long, with dropped handlebars and rigid front forks, and the Matchless relied on pedal cycle-type brakes on the front wheel and a foot lever and block on the belt rim to slow from over 70 mph for the many bends.

Since 1907 interval starts have been used for the TT Riders' start, in pairs or singly, and the riders are placed according to their elapsed time, not their position on the road. Although frustrating for spectators, who cannot tell what is happening without a commentary, and nerve-racking for a fast finisher, who may have to wait half an hour to know whether he has won or not, this is the only safe way to launch up to 100 racing motorcycles on to a narrow, wall-lined circuit.

An historic winner. Rem Fowler stands modestly behind the Norton-Peugeot V-twin on which he won the Twin-Cylinder race in the first TT. He raced again in 1908–1911, but never finished higher than 16th. **(BBC Hulton Picture Library)**

The coast road between Kirk Michael and Peel, 1910. Scout Marshals warn the Scouts on the next bend that a rider is approaching. The TT was a compulsory duty for every Isle of Man Scout until 1939, as marshals, messengers or scoreboard attendants. **(EMAP)**

Harry Collier swings through Peel on his way to winning the 1909 race. Spectator control was not a problem on the St John's Course. **(Manx Museum)**

Another rider comes to grief on the 'Wall of death' at Ballacraine. The wooden banking was only used in 1910 and riders soon learned to keep well clear of it. The idea came from continental road races, where similar banking was sometimes used. The rider is Eric Myers (Scott). **(EMAP)**

Approached on a swift, bumpy, downhill track, the Devil's Elbow tested the rider's nerve and his machine's stirrup brakes. A foot-down technique was normal on the loose surface. **(Colonel Mylchreest collection)**

Jack Marshall astride the Triumph on which he won the single-cylinder class in 1908 after a race-long battle with Charlie Collier. (Colonel Mylchreest collection)

A modern view of the Devil's Elbow, on the Kirk Michael to Peel coast road. Little has changed since 1907 except the quality of the surface.

The Tourist Trophy, awarded by the Marquis de St Mars in 1907. It represents Mercury, messenger of the Gods, riding a winged wheel. Replicas of the Trophy are given to winners and the higher finishers to this day. **(VMCC)**

Chapter 3:

Up the Mountain 1911–14

'This ain't gonna be no tea party' – *Jake de Rosier, Indian works rider.*

After the 1910 TT the ACC were persuaded that tougher measures were necessary to accelerate the development of touring machines, and crucial changes were made for 1911. Firstly the course was moved to the 37½-mile 'Mountain' course used for car racing since 1904. Secondly, separate 'Senior' and 'Junior' races were planned, with engine capacities of 595cc and 340cc for multis and 500cc and 300cc for singles. Neither change was widely popular and many riders reasonably argued that 70 mph down the mountain with no clutch and only stirrup and dummy rim brakes was an invitation to disaster. The prospect of slogging up the other side with hefty leg-work to keep above stalling speed cannot have been very cheerful either.

The move was made, however, and undoubtedly saved the TT from an early death. The new course followed today's circuit almost exactly, though a different route led into and out of Douglas. The road surfaces were narrow and unpredictable; most were covered with macadam, smoothly rolled earth and stones, while the mountain 'roads' were farm tracks, usually two stony ruts separated by grass. High hedges hid the bends ahead from view, and wandering pedestrians, animals and horse-drawn vehicles were a great danger. Every lap in 1911 was an adventure lasting the best part of an hour, and a brutal test of motorcycle and rider. Juniors were to cover four laps and Seniors five.

In practice young Victor Surridge crashed his works Rudge heavily outside the Glen Helen Hotel, in front of the horrified eyes of his team manager, and was the first rider to be killed racing on the Isle of Man. Sixty-seven Seniors and 37 Juniors started, in spite of all the objections to the new circuit, and the Junior race was won by a Humber twin ridden by P. J. Evans. The entire Humber team of six machines finished the race. All but four starters used two- or three-speed transmission, by hub gear or two-speed countershaft.

The Senior TT of 1911 was a classic race, the Matchless and Indian teams being favourites, but strong Triumph, BAT and Rudge teams challenged. The American Jake de Rosier, Indian's board-track champion, made the fastest lap in practice after several crashes, and he led at the end of the first lap, followed by Charlie Collier. Then things started to go wrong for de Rosier, who fell again, and made repairs with parts obtained from his refuelling station, contrary to regulations. Collier went in front, chased by four 'Red' Indians until he ran out of fuel and had to refuel away from the pits. By hard, foot-down cornering and sheer determination, Collier regained second place from Franklin's faster Indian, but he was disqualified for unauthorized refuelling. To the dismay of the patriotic crowds and British manufacturers, Indians swept the board, led by O. C. Godfrey, a victory well merited by the Indian's advanced design and strong construction. The Indians had all-chain drive with a clutch and two-speed gearbox, a strong and simple loop frame, and an external contracting rear wheel brake.

The fastest lap, at 50 mph, was made by a Scott two-stroke twin ridden by Frank Philipp. This advanced and elegant machine was water-cooled, had two-speed chain drive and a rotary inlet valve, but all three works Scotts lost the timing of these valves and retired.

After the TT the Indian-Matchless battle continued at Brooklands, where Jake de Rosier and Charlier Collier fought out three match races on the motorcycles that they had used for the TT. Rosier won the first race at 80.59 mph, surprising Collier by slipstreaming him for most of the race. Collier won the second after de Rosier's front tyre punctured at high speed, and de Rosier won the third race, slipstreaming until the last moment again. De Rosier tried to persuade Collier to return to the States with him, where his board-track racing earned him $300 (equal to £60 in 1911) a week, 'a veritable gold mine', but Collier declined. De Rosier died in 1912 after a board-racing crash, and no American of comparable talent raced in Europe until the 1970s.

1912–1914

> 'A. G. Fenn retired on the first day owing to his back spindle breaking. H. C. Mills had his flywheels come loose, while Clifford Wilson came off at over 60 mph owing to his handlebars becoming detached from his machine' – *The Motor Cycle* report, 1913.

The 1912 Junior was the first TT to be started in foul, wet conditions. The Douglas team soon took charge, first Bailey then W. H. Bashall leading on their lightweight flat twins. Water got in everywhere, and Bashall finally tired of stopping to dry his plugs and tried to dry them on the move, getting numerous lively shocks in the process. Bashall won, nevertheless, and Douglas machines were also second and third.

The Senior TT saw the Scott company's finest hour. With gears in place of chain drive to the rotary inlet valve, the two-stroke twin of Frank Appleby led from start to finish, making fastest lap and heading the second finisher, J. K. Haswell (Triumph), by almost seven minutes.

Before the 1912 races 20 manufacturers who disliked the rules and the location of the TT signed an agreement not to support it and in their absence Douglas and Scott won famous victories and gained immediate and substantial increases in sales. The lesson was clear to see and no fewer than 103 Seniors and 46 Juniors entered the lists for the 1913 TT.

The 1913 Junior and Senior races were lengthened to six and seven laps respectively, each race being split into two parts to be raced on different days. This complicated and unpopular arrangement was not repeated, but both races provided close and exciting contests. In the Junior, Hugh Mason pushed his low-slung NUT V-twin ahead of a gaggle of Douglas flat-twins and won by less than a minute from W. F. Newsome (Douglas), who had been shadowing a slower rider in the belief that he was Mason.

In the Senior young 'Tim' Wood rode with a grace and speed which anticipated Geoff Duke, to outpace strong Rudge and Indian teams. F. Bateman (Rudge) finished second on the first day of racing, but crashed fatally while leading on the second day. First to finish was A. R. Abbot (Rudge), but Wood had started after him and arrived in time to win by 5 seconds after over five hours of racing.

H. O. Wood (the 'Tim' was an abbreviation of his nickname 'Timber') had never raced a motorcycle before the 1913 TT but had shown his talent as a test rider at Scott's factory. His superb, smooth style was in contrast to that of the first and last Russian national to race on the Isle of Man. Kremleff, the Russian champion, seemed to forget that there were any corners on the course, reported *Motorcycling*, 'he approached most corners so fast that he had to make use of any escape road available, and crashed on the last lap near Hillberry.'

In spite of many road improvements and 22 large warning banners ahead of bridges and dangerous bends, there were many accidents and serious injuries in 1913. The ACU (as the ACC was now entitled) required riders to wear approved crash helmets for 1914, and the race returned to one day each for Juniors and Seniors.

1914

> 'If insulating tape was banned, how many machines would have finished?' *The Motor Cycle*, May 28, 1914.

AJS, the dark horses among the 14 makes entered for the 1914 TT dominated the race when the Enfield and Douglas twins faded away. AJS took first, second, fourth and sixth places, with two unrelated Williamses, Eric and Cyril, in front on their light, robust four-speed singles.

The Senior TT, with 105 entrants, boasted more different makes of motorcycle than any TT before or since: Motosacoche, Puch, NSU, FN and Indian entered works teams; Scott, Matchless and Sunbeam had completely new machines. Tim Wood raced ahead on the latest Scott, now with twin plugs for each cylinder, to be passed by Harry Collier when his engine began to misfire. Wood then gave up, Collier crashed at high speed near Sulby and Cyril Pullin came up to win ahead of six different makes in the next six places. Pullin's Rudge single, which used an expanding pulley variable gear, won at a record speed of 49.9 mph.

This was the last TT to be won by a belt-driven machine; even in 1914, seven years after the first TT, 'footslogging' at some of the steepest bends was accepted as normal. However, the mountain course had firmly directed motorcycle development towards all-chain drive, variable gears, reliable valve gear and strong frames with a low centre of gravity.

But it was to be a long time before motorcycles would race on the Isle of Man again. By 1920 the Collier brothers, co-founders of the TT, had retired, Captain Arbuthnot had gone down with his ship at the Battle of Jutland, and H. R. Davies had returned from a prisoner of war camp in Germany to read his own obituary.

Frank Applebee before the start of the 1912 TT on his Scott. The gear-driven rotary valve and the rear-mounted kick starter are clearly visible. **(VMCC)**

Frank Phillip reduces wind resistence as he accelerates away from Quarter Bridge during practice, 1912. **(EMAP)**

A fine view of Frank Phillip at Creg-ny-Baa in the 1912 Senior TT. Note the spectators' transport parked behind them. **(VMCC)**

Weather Changes, 1912.
James Stewart (Douglas) takes Quarter Bridge in sunshine. **(BBC Hulton Picture Library)**

W. Creyton (Humber) jumps Ballig Bridge in rain and mist during the same race. **(BBC Hulton Picture Library)**

L. S. Bailey (Douglas), in front of a good crowd at Parkfield, finds dry overcast weather. **(BBC Hulton Picture Library)**

Winner of the 1912 Junior TT, Aubrey Bashall was eliminated from the 1913 race by a crash at Ballacraine. His expression fits the situation. **(BBC Hulton Picture Library)**

Weighing in before the 1914 TT. The Senior Dunkley of G. N. Morris on the scales. **(BBC Hulton Picture Library)**

Ivor Hart-Davies makes an adjustment on his Triumph as he starts the climb out of Ramsey toward Snaefell. Note the very wide handlebars, which gave riders leverage to wrestle their machines through fast rough sections. **(EMAP)**

The start of the 1914 Senior TT. F. Greene and R. Poole (Royal Ruby) are poised to go, but F. Shakespeare (83) has found a problem on his BSA. **(BBC Hulton Picture Library)**

Farther down the line Harry Collier (right) and Jack Woodhouse, sitting on his Quadrant, wait for their turn.
(Colonel Mylchreest Collection)

Chapter 4:

Gathering Momentum 1920–22

> 'If the Tourist Trophy is to delay delivery, then the sooner the Trophy is abandoned the better' – *Triumph Motorcycle Co. advertisement, 1920.*

After the Great War too many customers were chasing too few machines for most manufacturers to consider there to be any advertising value in the TT, and for some the return to normal production after War Department contracts was slow. Only four factories supported the 1920 Senior: Norton, Sunbeam, Indian and AJS. The Scott factory promised great things for future races, but Triumph took out a full page in *The Motor Cycle* to print a pious justification of its absence and a condemnation of 'freak' competition machines.

So only 27 starters lined up for the Senior on 22 June, compared with 105 in 1914, but among them were some of the finest riders of the Vintage era: Freddie Dixon, George Dance, Tommy de la Hay, Graham Walker, Jimmie Shaw and the Alexander brothers.

George Dance (Sunbeam) drew steadily into the lead, followed by Alfie Alexander's swift, light, belt-drive Douglas and the Norton of Douggie Brown, then a fleet of works side-valve Sunbeams. Dance and Alexander retired in turn, leaving Brown to fight it out with Tommy de la Hay. Douggie Alexander remained in the race and finished sixth. At his second pit stop Brown was told to ease off as he was in front, but de la Hay pressed on hard to make his last lap a record (55.62 mph) to win by nearly four minutes. Eric Williams exited rapidly from the race through a (closed) wooden gate without injury to himself, Freddie Dixon's Indian hurled him along the road when his rear and only brake jammed as he came in for a pit stop and Graham Walker's front brake blocks jammed in his spokes, causing him to 'cast the model away'.

For 1920 the Governor's Bridge loop was included in the course, extending the lap length from 37½ to 37¾ miles and the start was moved from the bottom of Bray Hill to the Glencrutchery Road, near its present position.

The Junior Race introduced for the first time a 250cc Lightweight class, with a cup presented by *The Motor Cycle*. Eight AJSs started, six of them works entries, and the rest of the field of private Douglases, Woolers, Blackburnes and others were not considered serious competition. Four two-stroke Levises and three Diamonds contested the Lightweight cup.

At the end of the second lap, AJS machines held first, second, third, fifth and 13th places, with Eric Williams in front and R. O. Clarke splitting the phalanx with the strong little Levis. On the next lap, the three leading AJSs all broke down and Eric Williams held a short-lived lead until Cyril Williams passed him. On the fifth and last lap Cyril's AJS also broke down, with jammed gears, but by then he was so far ahead that he was able to push the last three miles home and still win by nine minutes.

The 1920 TT races were distinguished by bad brakes and brave riders. At least a dozen competitors were thrown off their machines by locked wheels, and most riders finished bruised and exhausted after a ride on loose, bumpy roads, lasting up to six hours for the slower finishers. The best brakes were probably on the Sunbeams, with substantial dummy belt rims front and back. The worst were on the Indians, with tiny dual back brakes only, ready to lock at the least provocation. One man made sure that starvation at least was not one of the discomforts of the race: S. H. Haden (Jr, New Comet) was reported to have stopped at the pits on every lap for a snack. Well nourished, Haden finished tenth.

1921

The 1920 races showed manufacturers how precious success in the TT could be in terms of increased orders. Norton, AJS and Sunbeam sales rose steeply after June, and in 1921 not four but 12 factories built machines for the Senior TT, among them the shameless Triumph company, and all hoped for a share of the spoils.

AJS returned to the 1921 Junior in force, aiming to pulverise the opposition with seven works entries. The AJS team took first, second, third, fourth and sixth places in the fastest TT ever run, but the fifth place finisher, Jim Whalley on the lone works Massey Arran, was well among the leaders until a last lap puncture, and actually took the lead on the third lap.

Eric Williams's winning time in 1921 was 3 hours 37 min 23 sec, compared to Cyril Williams's winning time of 4 hours 37 min 57 sec in 1920, one whole hour faster. The weather was fine for both races, so this staggering increase in speed should be attributed to improvements made by AJS to their racers between 1920 and 1921. These were many, if not visibly obvious, and included much stiffened valve gear, a lightweight, concave-headed piston and a three-speed countershaft gearbox with clutch. Each modification was thoroughly tested and proved long before the TT and the 1921 Junior average speed of 52.11 mph, faster than the 1920 *Senior* average, showed how formidable the little AJS was.

Two of the 350cc AJSs were entered for the Senior and were no doubt eyed nervously by the competition after their success in the Junior. Sure enough H. R. Davies, starting second in the race, passed the previous year's winner, Tommy de la Hay, who started first on a works Sunbeam, early in the first lap. At the end of that lap Freddie Dixon was first then F. Edmond (Triumph). George Dance (Sunbeam) and Alec Bennett (Sunbeam) each took a turn in the lead, while Howard Davies kept in second place with fast, consistent lap speeds. Finally, at the end of lap 5, Davies led the race by one second from Alec Bennett and then put in a fast final lap to win the race by 2 min 13 sec at 54.49 mph.

Dixon and Le Vack came second and third on Indians, the unlucky Alec Bennett finishing fourth – double vision and headache resulting from a practice crash forcing him to slow towards the end. First to finish in the Lightweight class, run with the Junior race, was D. G. Prentice (New Imperial), closely followed by G. S. Davison (Levis), later of 'TT Special' fame, and both handsomely exceeded the speed of the 1920 Junior winner.

1922

> 'The 66 men behind him resembled a flower garden in their garish colours – Indian red, Scott violet, Sunbeam black and gold, with the vivid grass-green helmets, jackets and breeches of the Rudge men standing out above all' – *The Motor Cycle*.

The man standing in front of this assembly before the start of the 1922 TT, wearing plain brown leathers on this sweltering summer day, was Howard Davies, hoping to repeat his 1921 victory, riding a 350cc works AJS again. But it was not to be; further improvements to the AJS motor did not save Davies from retiring on the first lap, and Alec Bennett took the lead on his Sunbeam and held on to it until the finish.

Bennett did not have an easy race, as he had to nurse an under-lubricated engine, but behind him his pursuers also had nothing but trouble. Harry Langman lost second place when he fell off his Scott, breaking a footrest, then he had to slow down to let his engine cool down. Walter Brandish, 21 years old, 6 ft 3 in tall and the darling of the crowd on the works four-valve Triumph, lost second gear but still finished in second place. Freddie Dixon, who had moved up behind Bennett when the Scotts overheated, had a puncture on the last lap. Graham Walker, who came fifth, recalled seeing Dixon near Ramsey 'jumping up and down on his rear wheel, with his arms stretched to the heavens and his mouth working with unheard oaths'. Freddie had gone to great trouble to improve his factory Indian to his own standards, but a hole in his tyre put his work to naught. After a very hot and dusty race the results were 1st, Bennett (Sunbeam); 2nd, Brandish (Triumph); 3rd, Langman (Scott); 4th, C. P. Wood (Scott); 5th, Walker (Norton). Only 22 of the 67 starters finished the race.

AJS duly won the Junior race (Tom Sheard) and G. S. Davison won the Lightweight on a Levis, from which he had removed all but the most essential working parts to reduce weight, at a speed which would have given him third place in the Junior TT.

Tommy de La Hay (Sunbeam) cuts a rough and dusty corner so close that he seems to be ducking the hedge. He rides without goggles in spite of the dust in the 1921 TT, in which he retired. **(VMCC)**

A fine study of mental preparation before the 1921 Senior TT. Bert le Vack concentrates his mind on the challenge ahead. He was to finish third. **(Colonel Mylchreest collection)**

Manxman Douggie Brown (side-valve Norton) before the start of the 1921 Senior. Behind him is Jack Emerson (Douglas). Neither finished. **(Colonel Mylchreest collection)**

Alfie Alexander's fast ohv Douglas at Creg-ny-Baa while lying fifth in the 1922 Senior TT. (EMAP)

Sporting the woollen stockings and heavy shoes that he preferred to boots, Jimmy Shaw passes the crowds at Governor's Bridge on a side-valve Norton. His best TT result in ten years of competing was fourth in the Senior in 1927. (EMAP)

Two prima donnas in one racing team caused tension in the Sunbeam camp in 1922. 1920 Senior winner de La Hay (above) felt that seniority should make him team leader; Alec Bennett claimed to be the better rider. De La Hay retired and Bennett won. **(Keig)**

Norton entered an experimental overhead valve machine in the 1922 TT. Although it did not finish, it was the basis of the Model 18 that flourished for 30 more years. Ralph Cawthorne looks cool about his prospects during practice. **(Keig)**

Chapter 5:

A Golden Age 1923–27

1923

> 'For sheer skill and nerve the Senior TT riders must receive the greatest praise. Their task was rendered doubly difficult by the adverse atmospheric conditions prevailing' – *The Motor Cycle*.

In other words, it rained cats and dogs throughout the 1923 Senior, the first wet TT since 1912. There were other excitements that year and total entries for the race were a record 177, most of them works machines. AJS failed to win the Junior TT and there was a race for sidecars.

Stanley Woods, only 19 years old, won the Junior on a Cotton after Jimmy Simpson (AJS), George Dance (Sunbeam) and Bert le Vack (New Imperial) all retired. Simpson crashed heavily avoiding a stray dog and George Dance, as he often did, blew up. Simpson made record lap at 59.59 mph.

In the Lightweight four-strokes outclassed the Levises and J. A. Porter won on a New Gerrard.

The Sidecar TT was a mixed success. Spectators were thrilled, if not horrified, to see sidecar wheels lift a foot off the ground on fast left-handers as the passenger climbed all over the outfit. Harry Langman (Scott), and his passenger showed daring beyond common sense, leading the race for two out of the three laps until an error by the sidecar passenger led to a violent crash at Braddon Bridge, fortunately without serious injury. Freddie Dixon now took over the lead with a banking sidecar that he had designed himself, attached to a works Douglas, and with his passenger sitting inside the sidecar throughout, he sailed home to his first TT victory.

The Douglas factory had a radical new machine for 1923, the model RA, which was light, low-slung and handsome. Among its features were a crude form of disc brake, dual balanced carburettors and twist-grip throttle control. Thirty-five RA Douglases were sent to the Isle of Man for riders in the Senior, Junior and Sidecar races and nine actually started in the Senior. This was a dangerous and uncomfortable race, in increasingly heavy rain and mist. Among many accidents and retirements was a fatal crash suffered by J. Veasey after his handlebar touched the wall at Greeba bridge. Most riders rode without goggles, soaked through, and G. S. Davison described his relief at breaking down at Ramsey. Tom Sheard was the fastest survivor, at a speed of 55.56 mph for 4 hrs 4 min, on a Douglas, and Norton won the Team prize.

1924

In 1924 it was Norton's turn to saturate the Senior entry list, with four works riders and six very able private owners, one of them Joe Craig, making his first TT appearance. Alec Bennett was now in the Norton team following a disagreement with Sunbeam team-mate Tommy de la Hay as to who was 'number one' in the team. Bennett won the 1924 Senior by maintaining a steady speed while Freddie Dixon tore ahead until his Douglas broke down. Second place went to that very gritty rider, Harry Langman, on a Scott. There were no official works Sunbeam, Douglas or Triumph entries, and the dreaded term 'freak machines' was heard again. Several serious crashes in 1923 made *The Motor Cycle* criticize the dangerously high speed of 500cc racing machines and even question the future of the Isle of Man as a race course, not for the first or last time.

In the event all was sweetness and light in 1924. There were no serious injuries, there were huge crowds and *The Motor Cycle* gave its lordly approval. It directed its scorn at the new Ultra-Lightweight class, for machines fit only 'for elderly riders and ladies', and more reasonably at the lack of team management in the Junior TT. AJS had apparently learned little from their experiences in 1923, and once again Jimmy Simpson roared off into the mist to shatter the lap record at 64.55 mph before breaking down. As leaders broke down one by one, an outsider, Kenneth Twemlow (New Imperial), moved up and was found to be the winner at the end of the race.

After a similar list of retirements, Kenneth's brother Eddy won the Lightweight TT, also on a New Imperial. In this race Wal Handley (Rex Acme) was the early leader and lap record breaker at 58.28 mph after the first ever massed start on the mountain circuit.

1925 was the last year that the 175cc Ultra-Lightweight class was run, giving Wal Handley his first TT win. It was 1951 before the Ultra-Lightweight class reappeared.

The Sidecar TT was also dropped after 1925 until its revival in 1954, and only nine starters in 1924 provided a mediocre race. Freddie Dixon and A. H. Alexander on Douglas outfits challenged G. Tucker and Graham Walker on works Nortons, Freddie rushing ahead with his banking outfit until his big end started 'clanking'. Alexander's big end also clanked, and George Tucker, who claimed to have sawed two inches off his handlebars to allow him to take Brandish corner faster than anyone else, came home the winner by half an hour.

The 1925 Sidecar TT was a much closer race, with twice as many starters. Dixon repeated his 'sprint and bust', but a Douglas, privately entered and ridden by 20-year-old Len Parker, won from two Nortons. Third finisher George Grinton was a very unhappy man, as he had been leading until a pit signal carrying a lone figure '3' misled him into believing that he was 3 minutes in front, and by prudently slowing he lost the 3 *seconds* lead that he actually held.

1925

Two main reasons are put forward for the demise of the sidecar TT. Firstly, manufacturers were discouraged by the very high engine mortality caused by the strains of sidecar racing, and, secondly, it was alleged that the antics and accidents of the racing outfits might put off would-be sidecar buyers.

The 1925 Senior should have been Alec Bennett's race. Bennett was a man who combined brilliant riding skill with a cool, calculating intelligence, and H. R. Davies, Stanley Woods and Wal Handley were among the few who shared those gifts. Nevertheless Bennett dropped his Norton at Governor's Bridge, and H. R. Davies, fit and fairly lean after weeks of body-building, won on the HRD built by himself and powered by a very special JAP engine assembled by Bert le Vack. Davies came second in the Junior too, to give his new company a magnificent TT debut.

Wal Handley won the Junior on a Rex-Acme, also JAP-engined, at 65.02 mph, much faster than the 1924 Senior speed; his lap record was 65.85 mph, and as well as winning the Ultra-Lightweight class, he broke both Lightweight lap records.

It was normal, at least until the 1930s, for riders, including those favoured with factory-build 'freaks', to be their own mechanics. Riders were usually accompanied to the Isle of Man by brothers, fathers or just good friends, who would help to repair damage done to a machine in practice, refuel and provide encouragement after a disappointing lap time. Most riders could and did rebuild and retime their engines at least once before a race, and many had little tricks of tune and assembly that they favoured. Each factory had its own base, often a shed or back-street garage, where work was carried out in exaggerated secrecy, helped along by endless cigarettes and cups of tea.

1926

£60,000 were spent on course improvements in 1922 and 1923, helping to increase speeds greatly by the mid-20s. Still more thousands were spent by manufacturers, who were setting up racing departments as if their lives depended on it. Twelve factories sent teams for the 1925 Senior TT; 16 entered the 1926 race.

Foreign interest in the TT had been slight in most years, except of course for the strong participation of the Indian company of Springfield, Massachusetts. Peugeot entered two fast parallel twins in 1924, and individuals like V. Naure (Spain) and Achille Varzi (Italy) entered British machines from time to time. Varzi was back in the Isle of Man again in 1926, and so was Tazio Nuvolari, later to become his most bitter rival in automobile Grand Prix racing. Unfortunately Nuvolari, who was with the Bianchi team, was not allowed to race as he had recently cracked his wrist, but Varzi finished an excellent seventh in the Senior TT on a Sunbeam. Bianchi and Moto Guzzi both sent teams, and 1926 was the first of 25 years of successful participation by the Moto Guzzi firm.

Norton won the Senior, Stanley Woods leading

five of the seven laps to which the race had been lengthened. J. H. Simpson led the first two before retiring, and poor Freddie Dixon did not complete a lap before the dreaded clanking was heard. Guzzi rider Pietro Ghersi greatly impressed in his first TT, finishing second in the Lightweight before being disqualified for using a plug not specified in his entry, and running fourth in the Senior before he retired. Stanley Woods just exceeded 70 mph to create a new Senior lap record, Alec Bennett introduced Velocette to the TT with a resounding Junior victory, and Cottons took the first three places in the Lightweight after Ghersi's exclusion.

1927

> 'In 1927 Howard Davies had a stroke of luck. The most exceptional, nay extraordinary rider of all time, the one and only Freddie Dixon, volunteered to ride an HRD' – C. E. Allen, *Motorcycle Sport*.

A man of unusual physical and mental toughness, Dixon was looking for a machine with strength to match his own. He obviously found this in the HRDs, for he actually finished in both Senior and Junior races, though in both events he managed to wrench the gear-lever clean off in his enthusiasm.

First to start in the Junior was George Reynard (Royal Enfield), who led on the road from start to finish, giving rise to comments about the fox and the hounds. First on time on lap 1, and on every subsequent lap except the last, was Wal Handley, riding brilliantly, and increasing his lead over Dixon on every circuit. Behind the two leaders Alec Bennett moved up to third place on his Velocette, to be replaced by Jimmy Simpson when his engine gave up.

A new electric scoreboard should have kept everyone informed of these developments, but it broke down, and the loudspeaker commentator attempted to report on every individual's progress in a high-pitched babble. This caused uproar among the spectators, who were treated to music instead, and the strains of 'In a Monastery Garden' could be heard between the roar of passing machines.

The last lap of the Junior brought joy to Dixon and frustration to Handley and Simpson. Wal's piston collapsed, ending his race, and Jimmy Simpson found another dog – and hit it, losing second place to H. Willis. One can only imagine the celebration enjoyed by Dixon and Howard Davies that night.

Norton and AJS brought brand new overhead camshaft engines to the Isle of Man for the 1927 Senior. The Norton, designed by Walter Moore and designated the CSI, used shaft and bevel gears to drive its single ohc, while the AJS used a chain enclosed in the shapely case familiar over 30 years later on the 7R 'Boy Racer'. AJS, Blackburne and Velocette also produced ohc engines, as did the incredibly low, water-cooled Tinkler.

The weather was not good at the start of the 1927 Senior, and although most of the course dried up, the famous Mountain mist persisted. This did not stop Stanley Woods from breaking the lap record from a standing start and tearing ahead on his ohc Norton. Freddie Dixon barged through in second place, here a broadside skid, there a bounce into and out of a gutter, and slower riders were wise to keep out of his way. At his pit it was 'a swallow of champagne and Freddie's off' according to *The Motor Cycle* of the day, but it was not to be a champagne occasion this time, for Freddie overdid the gear-lever wrenching and struggled home to sixth place.

Stanley Woods's clutch failed on the fifth lap, and it was Alec Bennett's Norton that won. His fourth win in 12 TTs was once more the result of a calculated race. Second was Jimmy Guthrie, a complete 'dark horse' at that time, though Bert le Vack's design and preparation of his New Hudson must have helped in his excellent ride. Tommy Simister was a battered third on a Triumph, his loyalty as a Triumph agent preventing him from expressing his feelings about falling off twice due to poor steering.

Alec Bennett's average speed was 68.41 mph, not much faster than Dixon's Junior speed. Wal Handley won the Lightweight race, leading every lap, and was followed by Arcangeli (Guzzi) and C. T. Ashby (OK Supreme).

In 1927 the TT circuit was only officially closed to normal traffic on the days of the races, so that during practice the occasional car or van was out on early morning business. Archie Birkin crashed fatally when he came on one of these vehicles at high speed and, rather late in the day, the Isle of Man legislated to close the roads for practice as well as for the races in the future. Birkin's death was a bad blow to others than his bereaved family; he was a director of McEvoy motorcycles in Duffield in Derbyshire, and was riding one when he died; he was a very popular young amateur rider – part of the 'fun' element of the TT – and his crash led many parents to forbid a TT ride – if not motorcycling itself – to their sons and daughters.

In the first sidecar TT many entries were experienced solo riders, but novices with sidecars – and it sometimes showed!

Graham Walker nearly hits the wall at Braddan Bridge (1923). He still finished second on his Norton outfit.

The brothers A. and N. Tinkler nearly lose their Matador outfit at Ramsey hairpin in 1924. They too recovered and came third.

A. E. Taylor and C. R. Hirst get it right at Quarter Bridge in 1925. They took second place with their Norton.

'Pa' Cowley, so called because his son also raced, corners at speed on his Sunbeam outfit. Eyeballs were tough in those days. **(VMCC)**

Soaked to the skin, Tom Sheard looks glad to have finished the 1923 Senior TT on the new RA Douglas. Standing beside him is L. S. Bailey, the Australian-born designer of the RA. **(Keig)**

Below: *The ohv Norton won the Senior TT in 1924. Here Joe Craig stops for fuel. Alec Bennett, riding for his third different firm in three years, won, while Craig was 12th.* **(EMAP)**

***Paddy Johnson (Cotton) speeds past the Snaefell Gate, one of the man-made hazards that were gradually removed from the course, in 1927.* (EMAP)**

Below: ***Two Royal Enfield riders demonstrate the leaning-out style of riding during the 1927 Junior. In front is G. L. Reynard, who led on the road from start to finish, but was fourth in the race on time.* (EMAP)**

Superman or Dennis the Menace? Freddie Dixon won the 1927 Junior and was sixth in the Senior for Howard Davies. He is here on the 500cc machine, which is fitted with his own modifications: footboards, a backrest and a windscreen. Dixon disliked goggles, and once when race rules obliged him to wear them he just removed the glass. **(EMAP)**

Charlie Dodson trails a foot in the rain before falling at Keppel Gate during the 1928 Senior TT. He recovered and won the race with a battered Sunbeam and boots full of water. **(VMCC)**

Chapter 6:

A Serious Business 1928–30

1928

> 'Dodson finished in remarkably fresh condition, though naturally suffering from temporary deafness from the continuous roar of the Sunbeam's exhaust' – *The Motor Cycle*.

After beautiful weather for practising (on officially closed roads), the day of the Senior TT dawned wet and foggy. Conditions were even worse than in 1923, and an unhappy band of riders splashed off, most of them with unprotected eyes as goggles soon became useless. Even more miserable were the many spectators who had camped overnight or even 'slept rough' at their favourite spots around the course, protected only by a mac and a 'flat 'at'.

The race was a disaster for practically everyone. Freddie Dixon, Stanley Woods, Oliver Langton, and many others, fell off during the first lap, and Alec Bennett, Wal Handley and Jimmy Shaw retired with engine troubles. Jimmy Simpson rode as if the roads were dry and led by a minute after lap 1, two minutes after lap 2, and then his engine blew up. Charlie Dodson took over the lead on a Sunbeam and Graham Walker, now riding for Rudge, moved up to second place, anxiously listening for sounds of distress from what he considered an under-lubricated motor.

On the last lap a few more riders skidded off the road, including Charlie Dodson, who hit a roadside verge on the mountain and gave himself and his Sunbeam a bad shaking. Graham Walker, still believing himself second, flogged his Rudge up the mountain, heard the hesitation in his engine that he had dreaded, and was out of the race while leading by three minutes. Dodson recovered and cruised home to win from a very pleased George Rowley (AJS) and a very bleary-eyed Tommy Hatch (Scott), who had misted-over glasses as well as wet goggles to contend with.

Alec Bennett won the Junior TT with the fine little ohc Velocette, setting the first ever over 70 mph lap speed for a 350cc machine. Frank Longman won the Lightweight with an OK Supreme.

1929

In 1929 motorcycle registrations reached the highest figure ever before 1950, over 731,000; competition to sell machines was intense, and manufacturers strained to succeed in the TT and increase their share of sales.

Ten factories sent machines to the Isle of Man, and some 'personnel management' (or waving of folding money) produced a number of shuffles between teams. Wal Handley left Rex-Acme and joined AJS, Jimmy Simpson left AJS and joined a powerful Norton team with Stanley Woods, Guthrie and Tim Hunt, and Alec Bennett changed back to Sunbeam, who had some of the machines most fancied to win the Senior.

Velocette surprised no one by winning the Junior (F. G. Hicks) at almost 71 mph. Moto Guzzi very nearly won the Lightweight when the popular Pietro Ghersi built a lead of three minutes, before retiring to give Excelsior its first TT win.

The faster 500cc bikes were now capable of a full 100 mph, and were no longer the greyhounds of the early twenties. Nearly all had saddle tanks, four speeds and foot-change, and a wide variety of sometimes complex overhead valve operation was in use. Although it was not actually raining when the 1929 Senior started, most of the roads were still wet after overnight rain, and there were evil, slimy stretches under trees. At one of these, three riders crashed seriously, one of them, D. Lamb, being killed; another, Wal Handley, bravely pulling him out of the way, while the third, Jimmy Guthrie, severely injured his leg. The race was extremely close and exciting for those able to follow the changes of position among the leaders. Relative newcomer Tim Hunt (Norton) and Tyrell Smith (Rudge) both led and fell off, the latter badly enough to be carried into a hotel, only to stagger out again and finish third with three broken ribs. Poor Graham Walker led again briefly until a push-rod broke. Charlie Dodson, however, stayed firmly in his seat to gain a secure lead over Alec Bennett, who came second five minutes behind, both on factory Sunbeams. Sunbeam took the team prize, four of them finishing among the 16 survivors out of 45 starters.

1929 was not a happy year for the TT. Two fatalities and a depressing list of injuries whipped up renewed objections to 'freak' engineering and the excessive speed of Senior machines. In addition factories were investing large sums in racing development, while at the same time steadily reducing prices, and often quality, in an attempt to increase sales. In 1921 the dearest Sunbeam cost 171 guineas and the cheapest BSA was £75. In 1929 the dearest Sunbeam cost 100 guineas and the cheapest BSA was £46. The Wall Street crash was only four months away, as Sunbeam celebrated its second TT victory in two years. The prosperous, carefree years were over.

1930

> 'The fifth lap gave Wal Handley's bookmaker another excuse to visit the bar. Despite the heavy rain and mountain mist he waltzed round in 29 minutes and 44 seconds, to lead me by no less than 3 minutes and 49 seconds, poor Tyrell Smith dropping back with a mysterious loss of performance' – *Graham Walker*.

Graham Walker in his fine series of TT recollections 'Seen from the saddle,' gives a fascinating account of the 1930 TT races. As Sales Manager and a rider in every TT since 1920, he was deeply involved in the extraordinary technical and personal events that produced first, second and third places for Rudge in the Junior TT, and first and second in the Senior. An experimental radially disposed 4-valve 350 had been built and entered for Tyrell Smith.

Then the Managing Director of Rudge, John Pugh, ordered every last spare part to be used to assemble two more machines, one for Ernie Knott, one for Graham Walker. In the event this trio finished first, second and third, breaking the race and lap record comfortably, and Walker failed to crush the little 350 with his 15 stone-plus weight.

The drama for Rudge in the Senior was the last-minute addition of Wal Handley to the team. Handley had been entered by the Belgian FN company, but no motorcycle appeared, and by dint of some complex negotiations with the ACU, and the good will of the Rudge team, Handley started on a Rudge. As expected, Handley rode brilliantly from start to finish, in conditions which deteriorated from fine to foul, soaking and foggy. During the fine period Handley put in three laps at well under the 1928 lap record of 30.47 minutes, lifting the lap speed from 73.55 to 76.28 mph. The filthy weather of the last two laps caused another crop of accidents, happily with few serious injuries; the race was a disaster for Norton with only one rider, Simpson, finishing the race. Arthur Carroll had taken over from Walter Moore as chief designer at Norton, and had immediately redesigned and simplified the ohc racing engine. The results of his work were yet to be seen, and Walter Moore went to Southern Germany to take charge of the NSU factory at Neckarsulm.

The Manx Parliament granted £3500 towards overseas riders' expenses in 1930, and this was most successful. Riders appeared from Japan, Egypt, Iraq, Sweden and Hungary, as well as the more familiar Commonwealth and European countries. This was the last year that Achille Varzi raced on the Isle of Man, and his presence in 1930 after he was well established as a top Grand Prix driver showed a real affection for the Isle of Man. Like George Dance and Buster Keaton, Varzi's photographs show him to be a man for whom a smile was a sign of disgraceful frivolity.

Sunbeam entered a works team for the last time in 1930, headed by Charlie Dodson, with George Dance as chief mechanic and team manager. Displeased with the speed of the team's new member, Vic Brittain, during practice, Dance examined his number-plate minutely to see if he had caught up with any flies. Finding a squashed fly at last he congratulated poor Vic, who actually finished eighth in the Senior. Dodson came fourth.

Jimmy Guthrie won the Lightweight on an AJS at 64.71 mph.

Melting tar fetches off Tim Hunt, works Norton, at Quarter Bridge during the 1930 Senior TT. Hunt's short but brilliant career with Norton included winning both Junior and Senior TT races in 1931. Severe leg injuries sustained in the 1933 Swedish Grand Prix ended his riding career. **(Motorcycling)**

Chapter 7:

Nortons Take Over 1931–34

John Pugh, Chief Designer and Managing Director of Rudge, looked to a Rudge clean sweep of all three TT races in 1931. A new radial valve 250cc machine had been designed, and three of these went across to the Isle of Man along with the 350 and 500cc machines. The members of the works team shared John Pugh's confidence, for Rudges had beaten Nortons in the race just before the TT in Northern Ireland.

Bad weather during practice concealed what became clear once the Junior and Senior races were under way: that Nortons were faster, steadier and more reliable than any other machine. Tim Hunt and Jimmy Guthrie swept into first and second places in both races, and Stanley Woods took third place in the Senior as well. On his third lap Jimmy Simpson took the Senior lap record to 80.82 mph and Hunt's average speed in both races was higher than the 1930 lap records.

These convincing wins were the start of Norton's domination of the Senior and Junior TTs until 1939. Rudge could only follow the Nortons home and by 1933 the company was in serious financial difficulty and went into receivership. The Sunbeam company was also suffering badly from lack of sales after 1930, though their owners, ICI, kept the company ticking over, so that Norton's two main competitors were no longer a serious threat.

The Lightweight TT in 1931 went better for Rudge. Ernie Knott took the lead and was four minutes in front when a tappet slackened off on the last lap. He managed to finish by holding the push-rod in place, but his stop gave a surprised and delighted Graham Walker his first (and only) TT win.

For the next seven years Norton's overwhelming success obscured some intriguing technical developments and personal successes. The German NSU company sent three racing machines to the TT in 1931: they were Norton CSIs redrawn by Walter Moore. Husqvarna sent two of their hefty V-twins from Sweden, and for several years both these firms gained respectable placings on the Island, the best being Ernie Knott's third in the 1933 Junior on a Husqvarna.

Velocette, who had started the overhead camshaft trend in 1925 (though Peugeot sent a fine ohc parallel twin to the TT in 1924), brought a supercharged 350cc KTT to the Island in 1931, but did not race it, as Harold Willis's arrangement of the supercharger blowing into the carburettor created an alarming delay in throttle response. 'Whiffling Clara', as the machine was called by its designer, got as high as tenth in the Senior before a bit fell off the carburettor, a common cause of retirement.

AJS also suffered badly from falling sales and faded out of the TT scene until the later 1930s, when the company's new owners, H. Collier and Sons, revived the racing department.

The old firms of Excelsior and New Imperial managed to keep their racing departments active during the dismal 1930s and produced some fine innovative machinery. A New Imperial ridden by L. H. Davenport won the 1932 Lightweight TT: an Excelsior using a new four-valve push-rod engine won in 1933, ridden by a very happy Sid Gleave, from Charlie Dodson's New Imperial. This race ended in great confusion, as due to a misunderstanding, the roads were opened to the public before the last riders finished, obliging Tommy Span to weave his way through spectators on the Glencrutcherie road as he completed his last lap.

Frank Longman, winner of the 1928 Lightweight TT, broke his forks on the bumpy Bray Hill descent and stopped to rig up a repair good enough to cruise to the finish. The mended forks collapsed between Sulby and Ramsey and poor Longman was thrown off and killed.

A successful effort was made to keep Rudge racing

by a syndicate of old team members, led by the irrepressible Graham Walker. The group achieved good Lightweight placings in 1932 and 1933, and in 1934 they persuaded Jimmy Simpson to ride a Rudge in the 250cc race. Jimmy applied his skill and experience and won his first victory in 25 TT races. Perhaps he had finally learned to be kind to engines. This was to be the last TT won by a Rudge.

The following Friday Jimmy celebrated his 34th birthday, and finished second to Jimmy Guthrie in the Senior TT, two and a half minutes behind his fellow Scot; he had already come second in the Junior, nine seconds behind Guthrie. In 1934 Simpson, one of the great flyers of the TT, along with George Dance and Freddie Dixon, won six continental Grands Prix, then retired from racing to work for the Shell Company.

Between 1931 and 1934 Norton took first and second places in every Senior and Junior TT and five third places out of a possible eight.

Norton were achieving just the same kind of results in continental races. Their success stemmed from a profound belief by Bill Mansell, their Managing Director, that racing 'improved the breed', stimulated sales and was even a patriotic duty. In Arthur Carrol he had a gifted and practical designer who continually reviewed and improved the ohc engine; in Joe Craig he had a cunning, forceful team manager. The merits of the works riders need no comment, for with Hunt, Guthrie, Woods, Simpson, and later Freddie Frith, J. H. White and Harold Daniell, the team included the finest riders in Britain and Ireland.

It was only when one of them ran off and started racing Velocettes and foreign motorcycles on his own that Norton's problems began.

Pressing on, as always, Jimmy Simpson leads the 1931 Junior TT before mysterious engine failure brought him to a standstill near the Mountain Bungalow. A suggestion that he check for a choked jet allowed him to restart and finish eighth. **(Motorcycling)**

Perhaps the finest motorcycle racing team ever: from the right, Stanley Woods, Jimmy Guthrie and JimmySimpson after their 1-2-3 victory in the 1932 Senior TT. Joe Craig, Norton team manager, stands behind and to the left of Guthrie. **(Keig)**

During the 1931 Junior, H. E. Edwards swings his Rudge round Sulby Bridge. This is one of the spots on the course that is still much as it was 60 years ago. **(EMAP)**

After winning nearly every international race for Norton in 1931, 1932 and 1933, Stanley Woods felt he wanted independence and a change. In 1934 he rode a Swedish Husqvarna V-twin in the Senior, but did not finish. **(EMAP)**

Chapter 8:

Challengers from Europe 1935-37

'My success in the 1935 Senior was due almost entirely to the accuracy of my signals – aided of course by a magnificent Motor Guzzi and a bit of good riding!' – *Stanley Woods*.

Besides a cheery smile and a never-ending supply of toffees Stanley Woods brought a totally professional approach to his career as a racing motorcyclist. He was a brilliant rider, but he had seen many brilliant riders lose a TT by going too fast or too slow through lack of information. Stanley himself lost the Senior in 1927 while well in front, destroying the clutch of his Norton while building up an unnecessarily big lead, and after that race he determined to ensure that at least Stanley Woods would know exactly how far in front or behind he was.

So Stanley applied his intelligence to creating an accurate private signalling system, with one station at Sulby and one at Douglas, connected by telephone and manned by his brother-in-law Gordon Burney and Athol Harrison, an expert timekeeper. Woods credited his double wins in 1932 and 1933 to the accuracy of his signals, and in 1934 he lent his team to Guthrie for the Junior TT, claiming that it gave the Scot his 9-second victory.

For 1935 Woods arranged to ride Moto Guzzis in both Senior and Lightweight races. The Senior machine was a 120-degree wide-angle V-twin designed in 1933, now formidably fast, and in 1935 the Guzzi had very effective rear suspension. Norton, New Imperial, Vincent-HRD, Jawa and AJS all entered works teams. In practice it became clear that the race would be between Woods and Jimmy Guthrie, and so it proved.

Starting first with number 1, Jimmy Guthrie set out to create a lead that Stan Woods, starting number 26, would be unable to close. He broke the lap record by 29 seconds on the first lap, broke it again on the second, and averaged 85.56 mph on the third lap to shatter it once again. Jimmy's speeds on an unsprung Norton, on a course that still had its wicked bumps, put him firmly among the ranks of heroes of the TT.

At the end of the third lap Guthrie and Woods came in to refuel, and the Scot had extended his lead to 52 seconds. Guthrie set off again extremely fast. Woods set off again, even faster, and now increased his speed to start whittling down Guthrie's lead. The Guzzi had lapped the North African race course at Tripoli at 111 mph and was now visibly the fastest motorcycle ever seen on the Isle of Man. Woods's descent of Bray Hill, incredibly fast but with both wheels sticking to the road, was a revelation. However, there was a rumour that the Guzzi would need to stop before the last lap and, sure enough, the Guzzi pit was prepared for refuelling; in any case Guthrie started his lap 26 seconds ahead, more than any man could make up at these speeds. Guthrie roared home after seven laps, and waited confidently for Woods to finish, Woods having started 14½ minutes later. Anticipating a stop to refuel by Woods, Jimmy eased off slightly on his last lap, 26 min 40 sec compared to his record 26 min 28 sec, on a signal from his crew. But the Guzzi did not stop. Stanley was signalled at Governor's Bridge earlier than expected and four seconds *within* the interval between his and Guthrie's start, Woods screamed across the finish line, absolutely flat out. Woods had averaged 86.53 mph (26 min 10 sec) on his last lap to shatter the record, and astound poor Jimmie Guthrie.

Whether the careful preparation of the Guzzi pit for a last-lap stop was a clever manoeuvre, or Stanley simply read his signals and took a chance, no one really knows. The most exciting TT ever ended on a slight note of mystery. Guthrie had some consolation in knowing that he had comfortably won the Junior in front of his new Norton team-mates, Walter Rusk and J. H. White. The three were followed by a trio of works Velocettes.

Woods took the Lightweight trophy with a 250cc Guzzi. One of his team-mates, Omobono Tenni, was a newcomer to the Isle of Man, a superb rider who disputed second place with Tyrell Smith (Rudge) until he fell at Creg-ny-Baa and damaged his Guzzi. The third Guzzi rider was Stanley Woods's brother-in-law, G. Burney, taking a rest from his signalling duties.

1936

Stanley's two wins with rear-sprung machines had a dramatic effect on everyone who saw them. Norton and Velocette developed new sprung frames for 1936 as well as modifying their engines. AJS entered two hefty supercharged but unsprung V-four machines; NSU, Husqvarna and DKW all entered works teams; New Imperial entered a single unsprung 500cc V-twin. Guzzis were absent, as Mussolini required all hands to build an Italian Empire in Abyssinia, so Stanley Woods needed to find a machine for 1936. He chose to ride for Velocette in the Senior and Junior races, and helped them to develop the new spring frame, and for the 250cc race he opted for one of the complex supercharged DKW 'split singles'.

Woods didn't last a lap in the 1936 Junior TT, the Velocette breaking its valve mechanism, and Jimmy Guthrie led until his chain came off at Hillberry. The lead was then taken, and the race won, by Freddie Frith, new to the Norton team, who showed the very highest skill in his first TT. Although Guthrie finished second, he was relegated to fifth place in the results after a confused dispute about the assistance that he had received to re-start at Hillberry. Guthrie's semi-disqualification was the sensation of the Junior to the Press of the day. The real sensation, however, was the fast and stylish riding of Frith in his first professional race, to average just over 80 mph.

Stanley also retired in the Lightweight, having led until the last lap and broken the lap record on his DKW. Another DKW, ridden by little Arthur Geiss from Germany, was third, but the winner was Bob Foster on a push-rod New Imperial. This was New Imperial's brief moment of glory, the last Lightweight TT ever won by a British machine.

The Guthrie-Woods battle was re-opened in the Senior TT. This time Stanley was the hare, starting No 2, and Guthrie the hound, starting No 7. The Norton had a little more speed than the Velocette, and Woods was unable to get in front in spite of 'scratching' all he could. Nevertheless, each rider was determined to win and the race was in doubt until Guthrie sped past the finish 14 seconds inside Stanley Woods's time. Woods's last lap was the fastest of the race, in spite of a misfire, but this year there was no easing up by Guthrie on his last lap.

1937

Once again, in 1937, the two great riders contested the lead. Guthrie started first and set a pace Woods could not equal, finishing the fourth lap 19 seconds ahead at an average well above the 1936 lap record. Then Guthrie's engine failed on his way up the mountain, letting Woods into the lead – but only 10 seconds in front of Frith, who had quietly been matching the speed of the masters. On completing the sixth lap Frith exactly equalled Woods's elapsed time, a dead heat after 2½ hours at 87 mph. Frith had been signalled his position and his last lap was a fantastic 90.27 mph. With both foot-rests and his exhaust pipe well scraped, Frith won by 15 seconds.

There were other magnificent performances in 1937. Jimmy Guthrie won the Junior at record speed, his last TT victory, for in August he crashed fatally while leading the German Grand Prix; he was greatly missed.

The Italian Omoboni Tenni emerged as a man of courage and vitality, whose ride on a Guzzi V-twin in the Senior was fast as well as hair-raising. Tenni was reckoned fastest of anyone at Hillberry, if one dared to look. In a very fast lightweight TT the DKW showed a new turn of speed, Kluge leading after one lap, then chasing Stanley Woods's Guzzi until retiring on lap 3. Then Woods also retired and Tenni won at 74.72 mph.

The DKW company was an industrial giant in the 1930s, and its large racing department produced a variety of piston-charged and supercharged two-strokes between 1920 and 1940. On piston-charged engines, the air/fuel mixture was drawn into a separate charging cylinder at the front of the engine and compressed by a piston operated by the main engine crankshaft (or by separate chain or gear drive on later models) before reaching the working cylinders. In 1937 they built their most successful racer, the 250cc piston-charged, water-cooled, rotary valve type ULD. The machine was powerful and so noisy it was said that one could hear it in Liverpool when the wind blew in the right direction. From 1937 Kluge and team-mate Wünsche won most European 250cc races and Kluge took the 1938 Lightweight TT, setting the first 80 mph lap on a 250.

The BMW company, with a much smaller racing

department, also built a winner in 1937. Their compact and light shaft-drive 'boxer' twin with a Roots supercharger, was a handsome, intelligent design that went on winning races with little alteration until 1951. Jock West was lying fourth in BMW's first TT when a split tank deprived him of petrol; after a ten-minute push to the pits, he managed to finish sixth.

1938

> 'And for me the 1938 TT was over. Next day I had to return to the mainland and the humdrum way of life. Despite the disappointment of retiring in the early stages of the race, for some considerable time I walked on air and lived in a world apart' – *Les Higgins* in *Private Owner*.

Within ten years the TT had changed its character completely. In 1928 it was still believed that the purpose of racing should be to develop touring machines and deep concern was felt that the speeds achieved by the 500cc racers, laps of up to 70 mph, were highly dangerous. The TT had passed its zenith as far as numbers of factories entering machines, but ten companies still sent racers in 1928.

In 1938 there was no attempt to justify racing as a source of touring development. The 'freak' machine was standard, and racing developments had produced overhead camshafts, supercharged twins and fours and rear suspension, none of which appeared on the typical British road motorcycle. This remained a stolid, unsprung ohv or sv single, high in weight and low in performance. If anything, Britain lagged behind Germany, Italy, even France, in development and innovation of touring machines.

Yet there was tremendous public interest in the TT, even from non-motorcyclists, and the BBC steadily improved its coverage of the races. It was now an occasion for nationalism and hero worship. *The Motor Cycle* actually printed a 'British Supremacy Number' in the late 1930s, full of the successes of Nortons and Velocettes in far-off lands. Self-delusion was completed by the much-loved phrase 'racing improves the breed' repeated so often in the motorcycle press that no one could doubt it. This is not to detract from the work of the racing departments and still less from the wonderful riding of the works teams, British and foreign. The TT was still the leading motorcycle event of the year and Stanley Woods and Freddie Frith guaranteed its power to thrill. Three successive Senior TTs had been intensely dramatic – could a fourth possibly equal them?

BMW entered a full team of supercharged twins for Jock West, Karl Gall and Georg Meier, a very competent and amiable young rider. AJS entered one blown V-four for Bob Foster to wrestle with, and Norton and Velocette entered teams. Norton fielded Frith, J. H. White, known as 'Crasher' White for past mishaps, and Harold Daniell. The Nortons had new telescopic forks and several improvements on the new double overhead camshaft motor introduced in 1937. Frith was first to start, Daniell No 15, and Woods No 30. Stanley made use of his late start number to improve his signalling network by placing a third station up on the mountain. Using binoculars to spot and time riders approaching from a distance, the signaller could give Stanley his position and gap as he passed, instead of half a lap late as before. Frith took the early lead, at a steady pace, and Woods was able to gain steadily, by increasing his lap speeds, to go in front on the third lap. After refuelling Daniell also cracked up his speed and dead-heated with Frith. Warned of Daniell's acceleration Woods too tried to increase his speed, but a horrifying 100 mph slide just before Laurel Bank restrained his enthusiasm. Daniell just went faster and faster, ending with a scorching lap at 91 mph to win the race. Stan Woods was second, Frith, the last of the three to turn up his speed, was third less than two seconds behind. Jock West brought his BMW to the finish in fifth place, well behind 'Crasher' White.

The Junior Velocettes were faster than the Junior Nortons and Woods won easily from Ernie Mellors on a second works Velocette. Mellors beat Frith by seven seconds and continued to start an eighth lap when the flagman missed him. He was kindly stopped at Creg-ny-Baa.

E. Kluge won the Lightweight on one of the new DKWs, his lead of a clear 11 minutes being the result of fine riding as well as a fast machine. Six Excelsiors occupied the next six places and the team of 'Ginger' Wood , Tyrell Smith and C. H. Manders took the team prize on the handsome ohc rear-sprung works Excelsiors.

Unofficial timings carried out on the Sulby straight in practice in 1938 show interesting comparative speeds. They showed Jack West (BMW) as fastest at 130.4 mph; then G. Meier (BMW) and J. H. White (Norton) 121.6 mph; H. L. Daniell (Norton) 120.8 mph; S. Woods (500cc Velocette) 117.6 mph; S. Woods (350cc Velocette) 112.5 mph; S. Kluge (250cc DKW) 107.8 mph; H. Hartley (250cc Rudge) 94.7 mph; and M. G. Tyrell-Smith

(250cc Excelsior) 92.3 mph.

1939

> 'When told that Meier seemed to need quite a lot of road at the foot of Bray Hill, Stanley Woods replied, "Well he can have all of it, I shan't try to pass him there"' – *The Motor Cycle, 1939.*

The highly charged political atmosphere in Europe, where Mussolini had invaded Albania, the Nazis had occupied Czechoslovakia and Hitler was fuming at Britain's determination to protect Poland from annexation, was not obvious on the Isle of Man in June 1939. At ten bob per solo return ticket, the Isle of Man ferries were packed, and an extremely large foreign entry promised some interesting racing. In fact, most of the Italian and German riders were already well known and highly respected as riders and sportsmen. Georg Meier was consistently fastest in practice on a works BMW, but his compatriot Karl Gall once more crashed in practice, sustaining head injuries from which he later died. The great O. Tenni thrashed a supercharged Guzzi single round for the fastest lightweight practice lap (at 82.8 mph) and the Germans Kluge, Fleischmann and Wünsche also made very fast laps.

The German presence on the Island included eight DKWs (four Junior, four Lightweight), three BMWs and seven supercharged NSU parallel twins. Although the NSUs were the type that broke the World's Motorcycle speed record in 1951, and looked truly fierce, they were slow and unreliable. Velocette developed a superb blown parallel twin, shaft-driven, with counter-rotating, geared crankshafts to minimise torsion in the transmission of power to the wheel, all set in a very modern multi-tube sprung frame. Sadly it failed to live up to its nickname of the 'Roarer'. The AJS blown four was now water-cooled and nominally rear-sprung, with small plunger units. The Italian Benelli factory set one dohc lightweight single for Ernie Mellors to ride. Capable of revving to 9000 rpm, it was faster than most of the 350s on the Island, and was accompanied by one mechanic and Mr Antonino Benelli himself.

Norton had prepared no machines for the 1939 TT, as a new War Department contract demanded all resources, but Harold Daniell and Freddie Frith were allowed to enter and race their unmodified 1938 Senior and Junior machines. Velocette had to leave out the 'Roarer' and Stanley Woods, Archer and Mellors rode dohc singles for the factory.

Stanley Woods won the Junior TT after an excellent race in which Frith and Daniell were very evenly matched by Woods and Fleischmann (DKW). Daniell's Norton threw him off in Ramsey town on the second lap, but he recovered to get ahead of Fleischmann and gain quickly on Woods. Between lap 2 and the finish Harold caught up nearly 50 seconds on Stanley, who admitted that for once his signalling service nearly let him down. Woods won by 8 seconds, to take his tenth Tourist Trophy, four more than Jimmy Guthrie had won and five more than Alec Bennett.

The lone Benelli took Ernie Mellors to an easy win in the 250cc race, though heavy rain made it an uncomfortable race. Tenni led the first lap, but dropped back and retired with supercharger troubles. Mellors won by four minutes from Kluge (DKW) and Tyrell-Smith (Excelsior). The BMWs fulfilled all their practice indications of being very fast. They were probably capable of 140 mph, compared to the maximum of 125 mph from the Nortons and Velocettes, and Meier was clearly not frightened of the bumps and stone walls on the Mountain circuit. He led by 12 seconds after lap 1, and by 2½ minutes at the end. Jock West on the second BMW was 31 seconds ahead of Frith and Woods, his speed, like Meier's, closely controlled from the pits. Neither Frith nor Daniell achieved the speeds they had averaged in 1938, and Daniell's 1938 lap record of 91 mph remained unbroken until 1950.

On a glorious sunny June day, the last TT for eight years drew to a close. At the Senior prize-giving, Stanley Woods paid tribute to Meier's riding, which was praise indeed from a man who had competed with Freddie Dixon, Alec Bennett, Wal Handley and Jimmy Guthrie. But diplomacy and charm were among the many talents of this man, who did more than anyone else to give vitality to the TT in the 1930s. His racing career ended in 1939 after 18 years of racing and 37 TT starts.

'Freaks' certainly won the day in 1939; nothing could have been further removed from a touring machine than the blown AJS V-four or the DKW. *The Motor Cycle* strongly advocated a TT for production machines for 1940, but in the autumn of 1939 the German army invaded Poland and motorcycle sport came to a full stop. By June 1940, many of the leading riders were doing technical war work, or were in the RAF. Wal Handley, Sid Gleave and Walter Rusk were among those who died in action, but most returned for the first post-war TT in 1947.

Jimmy Guthrie waits to start the 1935 Junior TT, which he won on a Norton. **(Keig)**

Stanley Woods gets ready to set off in the 1935 Senior TT. Rival Guthrie has already started. Chief timekeeper E. Hebblewhite watches the crucial seconds. **(Keig)**

1936, the year Stanley Woods rode a works Velocette in the Senior TT. Jimmy Guthrie won and Stanley was second. He helped develop the rear springing that kept his wheel on the ground at Bray Hill. **(EMAP)**

The 1936 NSU, still based on the 1927 ohc Norton design of Walter Moore, was handsome and fast. German J. Steinbach came fifth in 1935 and retired in 1936. **(EMAP)**

Stanley Woods tried a works DKW in 1936, and led the Lightweight TT until he retired on the last lap. The spectators at Governor's Bridge hairpin are not sure where to look. **(Keig)**

The perfect style of Freddie Frith, seen at speed during the 1937 Junior TT. Between 1936 and 1938 he won two TTs, was second once, third four times and retired only once, becoming Norton's most valuable team member. **(EMAP)**

It was said that the two-stroke supercharged DKWs could be heard in Liverpool, so loud were their engines. Ewald Kluge takes Quarter Bridge on the 250cc version on his way to win the 1938 Lightweight TT. **(Keig)**

Heavy metal! Bob Foster hangs on to the supercharged AJS V-Four during the early stages of the 1939 Senior TT. Both he and Walter Rusk retired. **(EMAP)**

Stanley Woods flattens himself on to the tank during his last TT, the 1939 Senior. He finished fourth and won the Junior, in both races on Velocettes. (EMAP)

The 1939 Lightweight: Kluge on the DKW at Governor's Bridge. Kluge came second behind Ernie Mellors, who also beat Kluge into second place in the 1939 350cc European Championship. (Keig)

Full of confidence and enjoying the ride, Georg Meier takes Creg-ny-Baa on the compact supercharged BMW on which he comfortably won the 1939 Senior TT. Although he continued to race for the BMW factory until 1953, Meier never took part in another TT. (EMAP)

Chapter 9:

Post-war Austerity 1947–49

1947

> 'A short push, the engine fired – into the saddle – accelerate away – into second – pull down the goggles – up into third – slide back on to the pad, now into top and away we went bumping down Bray Hill' – *Les Higgins, Private Owner*.

In lordly manner the ACU offered to run the TT again after the war – if it was wanted! Riders, motorcycle agents and a couple of factories expressed their enthusiasm, and it was on, with a few interesting innovations. Firstly, races for standard roadworthy machines were introduced, the Clubmans TT races, with classes for motorcycles of up to 250cc, 350cc and 1000cc. Full equipment to manufacturer's catalogue was required, though lighting, stands and number plates were to be taken off before the race. Secondly, several races were run together, the combination of Senior and Lightweight being particularly unpopular, more because riders had hoped to enter both than speed differentials. Finally, the only fuel allowed was low octane (70/75) petrol from the national Pool, an insipid carburant compared to the 50/50 petrol/benzole used in 1939.

Only four factories sent machines: Norton, Velocette, AJS and Moto Guzzi, who sent one 500cc V-twin to be ridden by Freddie Frith and 'managed' by Stanley Woods. This promising entry came to an abrupt stop during practice, when the front brake locked at Greeba, throwing Freddie off heavily and breaking a bone in his shoulder. Other pre-war veterans fared better, and Harold Daniell, Bob Foster, Jock West and Les Graham had lost none of their fire. There were also many excellent new men, some of whom had done well in the 1946 Manx Grand Prix, and who included Artie Bell, Ernie Lyons, Ben Drinkwater and Ted Frend.

The large entry of Clubmen, 51 in all, circulated safely enough in practice to confound those who predicted that a horrible mess of broken machines and damaged riders would result from unleashing all these amateurs on to the Isle of Man. Many Clubmen's machines did break down because of inexperienced preparation, while the 'professionals' rode in constant fear of overheated pistons, 'cooked' by low-octane petrol.

The Junior TT, run in clear, blustery weather, was indeed an engine-killer. The entire works Norton entry retired with engine troubles, and Velocettes swept the leader board, finishing first, second, third, fourth, seventh and eighth. Bob Foster won at 80.31 mph, a very respectable speed compared to Stanley Wood's 1938 record of 85.30 mph.

AJS entered two entirely new parallel twins in the Senior. These were a design derived from a supercharged flat 'triple' drawn up by Harry Collier's draughtsmen and modified to run unsupercharged. Jock West and Les Graham had frustrating rides, West taking 84 minutes for his first lap (an average of 27 mph), as he suffered from clutch slip and misfiring, but he later cracked round at over 83 mph to show the potential of the machine. The 500cc Nortons swept the board, as Velocettes had done in the Junior. Artie Bell and Harold Daniell raced each other from start to finish, Bell leading by one second at the end of the last lap. Bell's last lap was not fast enough and Daniell was lucky to win by 11 seconds, with a very hot and tired engine.

The Lightweight riders kept out of the Seniors' way, and Maurice Cann and Manliffe Barrington fought throughout for the lead on their Moto Guzzi singles. By lap 4, Cann had enough lead to stop by the roadside, change a valve spring, and continue in the lead. Barrington closed the gap on lap 5, led by 2 seconds after lap 6, and roared home behind Cann by almost exactly their starting interval of five minutes.

The official result was a win for Barrington, although almost every amateur timekeeper put him 14 or 15 seconds behind. The official result stood, and the rest of the field trailed in almost ten minutes behind the Guzzis.

The Clubman's races passed without any serious crashes, all three classes starting on the same day. The Senior winner, Eric Briggs, stood out as a rider of talent; like Dennis Parkinson, the Junior winner, he rode a Norton International. The fastest Lightweight finisher, W. McVeigh, was disqualified when engine measurement showed a bore 20 thous over size, the result of an earlier rebore on his elderly Triumph single. This gave second finisher B. E. Keys (AJS) first place. The Clubmen were well satisfied with their new series, except for lack of practice time, and the 1947 races, well organised, sunny and free of fatalities, ensured the future of the TT for a few years at least.

1948

Frith's practice crash in 1947 disabled him for the whole season, and he returned for the 1948 TT, aged 39, with some doubt about his fitness. The great Omobono Tenni returned with a Senior Guzzi, Ted Frend joined the AJS team and Ernie Lyons rode another Senior Guzzi entered by Stan Wood. Huge entries were received for every class.

In 1948, AJS introduced the 7R, a robust machine with a chain-driven single ohc engine, which became an internationally popular production racer; 25 of these 'Boy Racers' were entered in the 350cc class.

The Junior TT started in grey, damp weather, which improved rapidly as Frith completely dominated the race. Although Bob Foster was never far behind, Freddie's speed and style were a delight to spectators. He won at 81.45 mph from Foster, followed by Artie Bell and Johnny Lockett. Bell was disappointed to do no better, as he felt that his Norton pulled too high a gear for the windy conditions.

Having made fastest lap in practice, Tenni was visibly the fastest rider in the Senior TT, leading by 29 seconds on the first lap and by 39 seconds on the second, from Les Graham on a factory AJS twin. Tenni's passage through fast sections of the course was as spectacular and violent as Frith's was smooth and controlled, but Frith's Grand Prix Triumph was completely outclassed by the Guzzi. Les Graham dropped out, and by the end of lap 3, Artie Bell closed Tenni's lead to one second after the Italian slowed with a misfire. Tenni then took firm hold of his machine and flung it round the course at 88.08 mph, to make the fastest and hairiest lap of the day, in the course of which he whacked the wall at Sulby Bridge and triggered a camera hastily abandoned by a terrified *Motor Cycle* photographer. Then things went wrong for Tenni; his misfire worsened and at a pit stop to change plugs he took on insufficient fuel to finish the race. His ninth place was a poor memorial to a great TT rider, for Tenni was killed later in 1948 while practising for the Swiss Grand Prix. Harold Daniell, Jock West, Ernie Lyons, Frith and Graham all retired, leaving Bell to take a well-earned victory ahead of Bill Doran, second in his first TT on a Norton. A 348cc 'Boy Racer' AJS ridden by G. Murdoch was fourth.

The Lightweight was again run concurrently with the Senior (starting after all the 500cc bikes had left), with the surprising, and successful, innovation of a massed start. Once again Cann and Barrington contested the lead, but Barrington had a new factory Guzzi, a curious almost horizontal 250cc parallel twin that Guzzi abandoned after 1948. Barrington led for two laps, then retired to let Maurice Cann avenge his controversial 1947 defeat to win by almost ten minutes from Roland Pike (Rudge).

Ninety-one Clubmen started in perfect weather, their number including 11 1000cc Vincent-HRD twins and a single 'Tranquil Tornado' – an Ariel Square Four rendered less tranquil by removal of its silencers – ridden by C. Howkins. George Brown (Vincent-HRD) made a lap at 82.65 mph and led until he ran out of fuel, at a speed which would have given him second place in the Senior TT. So J. Daniell (Vincent-HRD) won, with F. P. Heath (Vincent-HRD) second, C. A. Stevens (490 Norton) third. It must have pleased Howard Davies, Senior winner in 1925, to see a machine carrying his initials win a TT again.

1949

It should have been an AJS year; Les Graham led a strong young team of Doran, Frend and Bob Armstrong on 7R singles in the Junior TT and on the parallel twins (called the Porcupine for its spiky cylinder-head finning) in the Senior TT.

Like Frith, Graham was an immensely stylish rider, with a tense and tigerish racing crouch, and he swung firmly into the lead of the Junior TT, 19 seconds ahead of Doran and 23 seconds ahead of Frith at the end of the first lap. Then Graham's clutch gave up and Doran took the lead, to hold it for five laps, never more than 12 seconds ahead of Frith.

Frith was riding a Velocette with a new dohc engine, and was not going to risk his machinery with unnecessary speed. His judgement was correct, and Doran broke down on the last lap, while Frith put on a spurt to make fastest lap of the day at 84.23 mph.

Frith won every International 350cc Grand Prix in 1949, to claim the World Championship for himself and Velocette. Early in 1950 he was awarded the OBE for services to motor cycling, the first man ever to be officially honoured in a sport widely thought of as less gentlemanly than car racing, a fitting end to a great racing career, for Freddie announced his retirement at the end of the 1949 season.

Back to June and the Senior TT, the Norton factory had come to regard the Senior TT as their property, and Joe Craig, their racing team manager, watched Les Graham (AJS) and Bob Foster (Moto Guzzi) make some very fast practice laps without worrying too much. Bell (Norton) made the fastest lap in practice, started number one and was only seventh after the first lap. Only Harold Daniell's Norton was in the first five, for the lone Guzzi and the AJS were all faster, and all in contention for the lead. At the end of lap 3, Graham, Foster and Frend all dead-heated on time, then Foster increased speed and drew ahead. Foster was nearly a minute in front, setting the fastest post-war lap speed, when his clutch refused to clutch and he was out. Les Graham became leader to break down in turn only miles from the finish, so Norton won after all. Harold Daniell led J. Lockett (Norton) over the line.

The Lightweight TT was won by T. L. Wood on a Guzzi, one of six that started. Two Italian newcomers to the Isle of Man, Dario Ambrosini (Benelli) and Enrico Lorenzetti (works Guzzi), retired early in the race, and at the end, the indomitable Roland Pike was third, ten minutes behind the winning Guzzi on his Pike-Rudge.

The Clubman's races were reorganized into two separate sessions; am for 1000cc and 350cc machines, and pm for 500cc and 250cc machines, which allowed almost 170 clubmen to start. One clubman in the 500cc class started with an unfair advantage; he was the most brilliant racing motorcyclist of the post-war period. Geoff Duke left his opposition far behind in a display of smooth, forceful riding. 'His "out" from one corner blended into his "in" of the next bend,' wrote *The Motor Cycle*'s reporter, who wondered if Duke was really trying, even at that speed. Before the end of 1949 Duke was signed on as a member of the Norton works team.

Stanley Woods entered Freddie Frith for the 1947 Senior on this V-twin Moto Guzzi, seen about to set out on a wet practice lap. The Guzzi crashed when the front brake locked and Freddie's injuries prevented him from racing for several months. (Keig)

Winner of the 1947 250cc race, Manliffe Barrington, out in the country on his Guzzi single. (Keig)

Artie Bell won the 1948 Senior after Tenni's Guzzi slowed down. The full primary chain case seems a luxury on a racing machine. (Keig)

Determination in every muscle, Omobono Tenni accelerates away from Quarter Bridge while leading the 1948 Senior on his Moto Guzzi V-twin. **(Keig)**

A superb shot by Bill Banks of Tenni taking off at Ballaugh Bridge. **(EMAP)**

Bill Banks abandoned his camera on the parapet of Sulby Bridge to leap to safety when Tenni skidded on oil dropped at the bend. Amazingly, Tenni triggered the camera when his Guzzi hit the wall to obtain this unique picture. He managed to stay on his motorcycle and carry on. **(EMAP)**

Bob Foster drew ahead in a closely fought 1949 Senior TT to lead on his works Guzzi until he retired. This was Guzzi's first year for the leading link front forks that they continued to use until they gave up racing in 1957. **(Keig)**

Les Graham also led the 1949 'Senior', riding the AJS Porcupine parallel twin, but his magneto drive broke on the last lap and Graham had a long push to finish tenth. **(Keig)**

Moto Guzzi mechanics work on Bob Foster's V-twin Guzzi before the 1949 TT. Features unique to Guzzi at that time were the 'backbone'-type frame, a long rear damping spring under the engine, and the streamlined fuel tank. **(EMAP)**

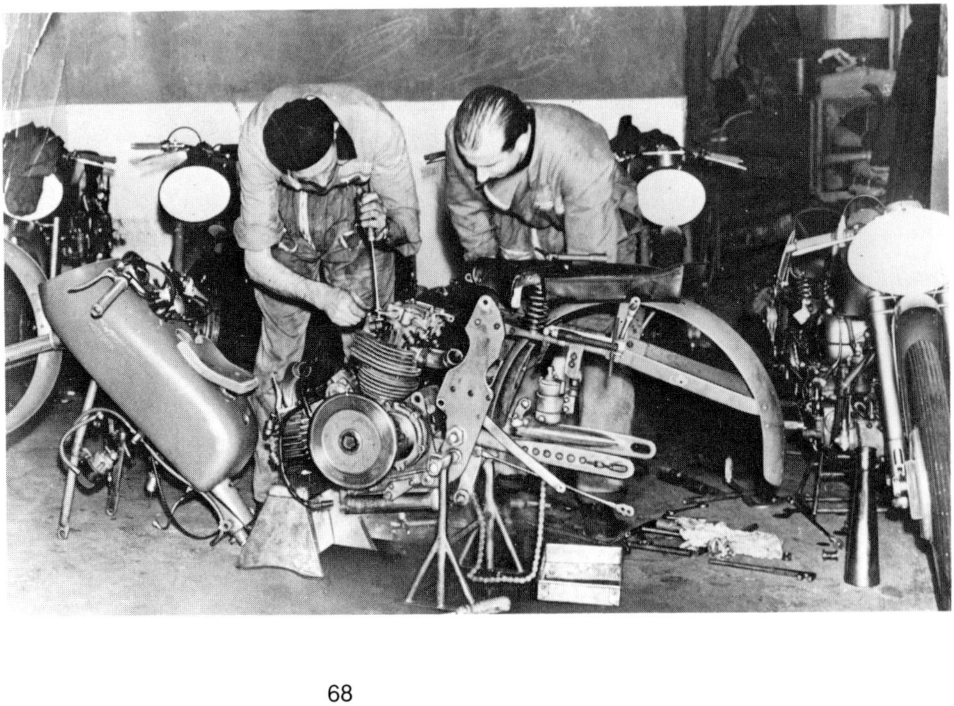

Geoff Duke winning his first TT, the 1949 Clubman's on a Norton 'International'. His graceful, efficient style is already noticeable. **(Keig)**

With the initials of Howard Davies still on the tank, the 1000cc Vincent HRD of George Brown sweeps round Quarter Bridge. He led, but retired in the first 1000cc Clubman's race. **(Keig)**

The post-war horizontally-opposed Douglas twin failed where BMW succeeded. The lower-set cylinders were prone to ground on bends and its transmission was turned through 90 degrees to give chain instead of shaft drive. This photograph was taken during the 1949 Clubman's TT. **(Keig)**

Chapter 10:

A Second Golden Age 1950–54

> 'My only real excitement arrived on lap 5 at the Highlander. The model took off, as usual, over the hump – doing about 125 mph. My feet left the footrests as usual, but unfortunately I missed the footrests completely when landing and only just managed to drag myself back on to the machine' – *Geoff Duke, 1950.*

The age of austerity in postwar TT racing ended spectacularly with the first 90 mph lap since 1939, made in practice by Geoff Duke on a Norton using 80-octane fuel. This was a Norton that looked nothing like the familiar machine that had won countless races between 1931 and 1949, with its strong hard lines and dominant tapering petrol tank. The new Norton had a smooth, rounded appearance that should have won it a design award, and although the engine was a strengthened version of the old dohc unit, its frame was completely new. Developed from a scrambler frame put together by the McCandless brothers and Artie Bell, it consisted of a duplex loop with pivoting rear forks, and it gave such a comfortable ride that the frame, and later the motorcycle itself, became known as the 'Featherbed' Norton.

The Featherbed Nortons dominated the Junior TT, winning at a new record speed and taking the first three places. Les Graham rode his AJS into fourth place, but Artie Bell won and set a very fast new record lap at 87.3 mph. He must have been delighted with his success on a machine in whose design he had played a part.

Bell went on to finish second in the Senior TT at over 90 mph. Sadly this was his last TT, for he was involved with Graham in a terrible high-speed smash in the Belgian Grand Prix which ended with both riders sliding into a timekeeper's hut. Artie had multiple injuries which finished his racing days; Les Graham escaped unhurt.

The new Nortons dominated the Senior TT as even Nortons had never done before, and the motorcycle press was at a loss to describe Duke's ability as a rider. Graham Walker, who had seen them all since 1920, doubted whether Alec Bennett, Wal Handley or Jimmy Guthrie could match Duke's finesse. His progress in the 1950 Senior TT speaks for itself, for he steadily increased his lead from 19 seconds after lap 2 to 2½ minutes at the finish, with a new lap record over half a minute faster than Daniell's 1938 time. Duke's speed was 93.33 mph compared to Daniell's 91.00 mph.

All four works Nortons finished, first, second, third and fifth, with Les Graham in fourth place again on a 'Porcupine' AJS.

In the Lightweight TT there was trouble for the Guzzis, in the shape of Ambrosini and his Benelli. This machine, with girder forks, looked exactly like the Benelli on which Ted Mellor won the 1939 Lightweight, and there was a strong suspicion that this was the same machine. Whether it was or not, Ambrosini made a poor start on it, then started catching up with Maurice Cann, who had been battling with Tommy Wood until Wood retired. In this, his second TT, Ambrosini rode ferociously and passed Cann within sight of the finish, his fastest lap of 80.91 mph being a new Lightweight record.

1951

> 'This year one of the [Norton] factory specials carries, of course, the phenomenon Geoff Duke.... His modesty remains intact after a series of intoxicating triumphs...' – *The Motor Cycle.*

Apart from illustrating the style now denied to us by the motorcycle press ('Hislop posts Proddie fastest, then crashes,' – *Motor Cycle News 1988*) the above extract was a drop in the ocean of praises poured on to Duke. He was 350cc World Champion, and only just missed the 500cc Championship.

The Norton team had lost Artie Bell and Harold Daniell, the latter retiring after ten battling TT years, so Duke led a new team, with Johnny Lockett, Jack Brett and the Australian Harry Hinton. Les Graham left AJS after 1950, having won the 1949 500cc World Championship for them, to ride for the Italian firm of M. V. Agusta. His machine for the 1951 Senior was a shaft-drive transverse four modelled on the successful racing Gileras, and in the absence of the usual Guzzi V-twin, his was the only foreign entry.

Geoff Duke won the Junior and Senior races unchallenged, and broke race and lap records in both races, with a new Senior record of 95.22 mph. There was no sign of a challenge in the Junior TT, in which factory Nortons came first, second and third, with an AJS and two Velocettes taking the next three places. It had been hoped that Les Graham on the MV or Bill Doran on the works Porcupine AJS might at least worry the leading Nortons, but Graham retired early in the race with valve gear trouble. Graham had a dismal year with MV, but he worked hard at development of the machine. By 1952 the MV had a lightweight loop frame and chain drive, and was a very competitive motorcycle.

Doran took second place, 4 minutes 20 seconds behind Duke, after Johnny Lockett retired. The other two works AJS twins retired, and although the Porcupine was developed and modified for several more years, it never equalled its achievements of 1949.

An interval start was restored to the Lightweight TT, unfortunately, making it harder to follow the Benelli-Moto Guzzi battle. Guzzi fielded a very strong team of Tommy Wood, E. Lorenzetti and Fergus Anderson, and Anderson flew away from the start to set a new lap record of 83.7 mph before breaking down. Ambrosini's best efforts were not enough to beat Wood, who won by only 8 seconds, with Enrico Lorenzetti third, 3½ minutes behind the Benelli.

Many riders of elderly British machines were embarrassed by the introduction of a 125cc Ultra-Lightweight race in 1951. Following immediately behind the 250s, many of the 125s overhauled the larger machines, and the winning Mondial won at a speed of 74.85 mph, ridden by Cromie McCandless, one of the instigators of the Featherbed frame.

The Clubman's TT races were won by BSA (Junior) and Norton (Senior) at speeds well below Duke's 1949 records.

1952

With Duke leading the Norton factory team in Junior and Senior TTs, there was not much doubt who would be the winner of these races. As for second place, this was wide open, for Les Graham was back with a completely new MV Agusta, and AJS had redesigned the 'Porcupine'. Suddenly there was a chronic shortage of experienced riders: only Bill Lomas, Graham and Duke could be called veterans of international racing, but a number of fine Commonwealth riders were appearing in the top rank: men like Rod Coleman (New Zealand), Ken Kavanagh (Australia) and Ray Amm (Rhodesia).

The Junior race was won by Duke at what looked like a stroll. He looked and even sounded slower than the second and third finishers, but he won at a record 90.29 mph with team-mate Armstrong second and Rod Coleman (AJS) third. The AJS was a new three-valve design, with two exhaust valves and one inlet; a complex design that was little faster than a standard 7R in good tune.

Les Graham made the challenge hoped for in the Senior TT, and when Duke retired on the fifth lap with clutch trouble, Graham took a precarious lead, only ten seconds in front of Armstrong. If crowd support equalled horsepower, Graham would have won, but he missed a gear-change, over-revved the MV engine and damaged one or two valves. Armstrong pulled ahead on the sixth lap and won, breaking his primary chain as he crossed the line. Graham followed, 26½ seconds behind.

The two Clubman's races were fast and furiously fought. Fastest lap in the 350cc class was made by Bob McIntyre (BSA), the first step in a racing career that was to include membership of the AJS, Gilera and Honda factory teams. The Senior race was stylishly won by B. J. Hargreaves on a Triumph twin; behind him K. R. V. James and D. K. Farrant fought a race-long battle to finish four seconds apart.

Fergus Anderson, a tall, cheerful Scott, led a very strong Moto Guzzi team of Maurice Cann, Sid Lawton, E. Lorenzetti and Bruno Ruffo. Ruffo, 1951 World Champion in the 250cc class, broke the 250cc lap record in practice with a speed of 84.33 mph on his first visit to the Isle of Man, crouching flat on the tank through bends where most riders sat up to slow down. Moto Guzzi, however, had a very firm team manager, Dr Parodi, who ordained that Anderson would lead the team home. There was no challenge from Benelli this year, for their star, Ambrosini, had crashed fatally on melted tar during the 1951 French Grand Prix. Les Graham on a lone 250cc Velocette was the only man who could possibly challenge the Guzzis. Anderson led on the first lap as planned, but then Ruffo refused to hold back and turned in two extremely fast laps, one of them at 84.82 mph, and flew into the lead. His fourth and last lap was ostentatiously slow, letting Anderson and Lorenzetti, and a whole lot of other riders, pass him, so Anderson it was who won. Les Graham finished fourth.

Meanwhile in the 125cc class, the beautiful tiny twin ohc FB Mondials were challenged and beaten by Cecil Sandford, riding the MV intended for Les Graham. Graham preferred to try his luck with the works Velocette in the Lightweight race and nominated Sandford to replace him on the 125 MV. Three Italian companies, FB Mondial, Morini and MV Agusta were the only serious contenders in the Ultra-lightweight class between 1947 and 1952, and Italian motorcycles also monopolized the 250cc class.

Geoff Duke, 350cc and 500cc World Champion in 1951, was 350cc Champion in 1952, and for his outstanding successes was awarded the OBE. He was also voted sportsman of the year, and for the first time, until Mike Hailwood appeared, the best-known sportsman in the UK was a racing motorcyclist.

Motorcycle sales in 1952 were booming. Motorcyclists could choose from an enormous range of engine sizes and types, from a 98cc James to a 1000cc Ariel four-cylinder, by way of singles, flat-twins, parallel twins, in-line twins and the Vincent V-twin. However, most of these designs dated from 1947 or earlier, and although development continued, British manufacturers seemed to be running out of original ideas – perhaps commercial success took away their urgency. In racing, development was falling seriously behind continental progress again.

1953

By the end of 1952 a major revival of interest in racing by European manufacturers was under way. In Italy Moto Guzzi were experimenting with a radical new four-cylinder racer with fuel injection and MV Morini, Mondial and even Lambretta fielded new designs. In Germany, NSU, encouraged by taking the World's motorcycle speed record in 1951, resumed racing with new single-, twin- and four-cylinder machines. BMW and DKW also re-entered international competition, giving several young German and Austrian riders their first experience of international racing.

The number of factory entries in the TT was greater in 1953 than at any time since the 1920s. Norton's team was without Geoff Duke, who had joined Gilera at the end of 1952, and open and exciting racing was expected. Gilera's powerful team also included R. H. Dale and A. Milani, but the factory had no TT experience; did it matter? Surely Graham was due for the win he had so often, so nearly, missed.

Two British riders of Italian machines worried the AJS and Norton squads in the Junior TT, one of them Fergus Anderson on a 320cc Guzzi, who finished third behind Amm and Kavanagh on factory Nortons. Clutch failure stopped Les Graham from making a threat with a new 350cc MV.

To the delight of all his supporters Graham won the 125cc race with a new lap record of 78.21 mph, a win at last after so many unlucky misses.

Moto Guzzi took racing so seriously that they built a wind tunnel to perfect the streamlining of their machines. The result was unconventional, but it was very fast. Fergus Anderson pushed past his only rival in the Lightweight TT to win at 84.73 mph. Second was an NSU ridden superbly by little Werner Haas on his first visit to the Isle of Man, and third was S. Wünsche, back with the DKW team after 13 years' absence.

All the promise of a great Senior TT turned to tragedy when Les Graham lost his life in an appalling crash at the bottom of Bray Hill during the second lap, while lying second to Duke's Gilera. The accident was apparently caused by a mechanic's error in reassembling the Earles front forks, so that they locked up when the forks bottomed on the hill. Duke fell off on wet tar at Quarter Bridge and Ray Amm, now the star of the Norton team, won by over a minute from Reg Armstrong's Gilera. A second rider, G. J. Walker from Australia, was killed when his footrest caught a kerb and he was flung from his machine.

The Gold Star BSA made its mark in the Junior Clubman's race by winning at 80.17 mph ridden by D. T. Powell; the Senior was won by the new Featherbed International Norton, ridden by R. D. Keeler.

No less than four fatal accidents marred the 1953 series, the worst year since the TT began.

1954

Sidecar racing returned to the Island in 1954. Not around the Mountain circuit as in 1923, when 'charioteers' last had a TT, but on a new 10.79 mile circuit, the Clypse. This circuit was introduced in an effort to please spectators by more frequent appearances of the racers, but although each competitor passed more often, small entries defeated its object. The Clypse turned right after the start before Bray Hill, at Parkfield Corner, and headed for Creg-ny-Baa in the 'wrong' direction, then turned right toward Laxey, turned right again at Ballacoar toward Douglas and rejoined the TT course at Signpost corner, to finish on the Glencrutchery road.

A fine overseas entry, which included the latest developments from the NSU, Moto Guzzi, Gilera and MV factories, threatened to overwhelm the surviving British teams from Norton and AJS. Fergus Anderson made some fast practice laps on the impressive fuel-injection shaft-drive Moto Guzzi 'four' and Guzzi also dominated the 350cc class in practice.

In the Junior race, the two Guzzis of Anderson and Kavanagh led after lap 1; only Ray Amm could keep within striking distance. On lap 2 he struck, with a new lap record that brought him absolutely level with Kavanagh in a dead heat for the lead, as Anderson had retired. This was the quality of riding that one had now come to expect from Amm, and when Kavanagh's motor began to 'clank' in the best TT tradition, Amm pulled ahead to lead by over a minute. But then Amm's motor also gave up and Rod Coleman scored an unexpected but popular win.

In the afternoon Moto Guzzi faced NSU for the Lightweight TT, hoping that rider experience would overcome NSU's mechanical superiority. The massed start saw the NSUs streak in front, and Fergus Anderson struggled up to third place, only to have his aluminium streamlining detach itself and slow him to fifth. The speed and regularity of the NSUs were awe-inspiring. All the riders had the same small, slim physique, and seemed to be products of the same factory as the motorcycles, and all five finished, first, second, third, fourth and sixth. Little Rupert Hollaus, the young Austrian, finished second at almost 90 mph in his first TT and was beside himself with joy at his success.

In the Ultra-Lightweight race over the Clypse Circuit Hollaus did even better. For ten laps he raced wheel to wheel with Carlo Ubbiali (MV), leading for most of the race, refusing to give ground to the experienced Italian, and in the last yards he nosed in front and won.

Among the spectators in 1954, one who was most impressed by the design and performance of the NSUs was Sochiro Honda, at that time in the middle of a massive modernization programme of his motorcycle factory in Japan. When Honda entered international racing in 1959, the influence of NSU was clear to see.

Eric Oliver, sidecar World Champion five times since 1949, led the sidecar TT from start to finish on a works Norton-Watsonian outfit, the first 'kneeler' to be developed and one of the first racing outfits to have motorcycle and sidecar constructed as an inseparable unit. Second, third and fourth were BMWs with separate bolted-on 'chairs', second place going to Fritz Hillebrand, a spirited ex-Luftwaffe pilot. The racing was not close, but the novelty of sidecar racing appealed to spectators.

The 500cc TT was a more serious affair. After much dithering, the stewards started the race in atrocious conditions, and in heavy rain the field set off towards thick mist over Snaefell. Many riders slipped off their machines, and Fergus Anderson escaped injury in a 120 mph crash that so shook Ken Kavanagh, who was following, that Kavanagh also retired. Geoff Duke took the lead on his Gilera at an astonishing 88 mph, his goggles gradually filling with water, but Ray Amm was the man of the race. With foot down like a speedway rider on the bends, Amm passed Duke to take the lead that he was still holding when the race was suddenly stopped after only four laps completed out of the seven. Amm was declared winner, and a strong Gilera protest against lack of warning of the premature finish was not upheld. What should have been a great race was rendered a fiasco by two bad decisions in difficult circumstances, but Ray Amm's incredible ride will never be forgotten. It was his last TT, for shortly after joining MV Agusta early in 1955, he was killed in a minor race in Italy.

The winning combination of Geoff Duke and the 'featherbed' Manx Norton at work at Quarter Bridge during the 1950 Senior TT. Reporters were lost for words to describe his devastating style. **(Island Photographics)**

Bill Doran finished second in the 1951 Senior after other race leaders retired. Here he is on the works AJS twin at the slowest point of the course, Governor's Bridge. **(Keig)**

Now at one of the fastest points on the Island, Bill Doran shoots down Bray Hill, head well down, in the same race. (Island Photographics)

Les Graham rode the massive shaft-drive MV Agusta with his usual verve, but it only lasted two laps. (Keig)

Les Graham and MV made many changes to the 500cc machine for 1952, chief of them being chain drive and an alloy frame with a leading link front fork. The improved MV took second place in the Senior race. **(Keig)**

In a year that was full of technical interest, Norton designed this streamlined 'kneeler' around the single-cylinder engine. Here Ray Amm flies it over the hump at Ballagarraghyn Bridge in practice. He used conventional bikes in the races. **(EMAP)**

A brilliant shot of Ray Amm, flat out down the high-speed swoop of Bray Hill on his way to winning the 1953 Senior TT. The true angle of descent can be seen from the spectators and buildings in the background. **(Island Photographics)**

Les Graham, tucked well into the MV 125cc single, heads for first place in the 1953 Ultra-Lightweight TT, his only TT victory. **(EMAP)**

Warming up for a cold race, the two most successful NSU team members, Rupert Hollaus and Werner Haas, before the 1954 125cc race, which Hollaus won. **(Dieter Herz)**

Probably the most overwhelming domination of a race by one team: the NSU team line up before the start of the 1954 Lightweight TT, in which they took the first four places. **(Dieter Herz)**

The 'Dolphin' streamlined NSU 250cc twin was faster than most 350s and a major step forward in racing design. H. P. Müller brakes for Quarter Bridge on the machine that inspired Honda. **(Keig)**

Fergus Anderson tried his hardest to split the NSU team, but could only manage fifth place. The damaged streamlining reveals the small-diameter space frame of the 1954 works Guzzi. **(Keig)**

H. Baltisberger gets behind the 125cc NSU's fairing on a fast stretch on the Clypse Circuit. The spectators seem more interested in their sandwiches. **(Keig)**

The first sidecar TT since 1925 gets under way on the Clypse Circuit. This is Parkfield Corner, where the Clypse Circuit leaves the Glencrutchery road before Bray Hill. **(Keig)**

Eric Oliver on the first ever 'kneeler' sidecar outfit, a works Norton-Watsonian, drives round F. Garrington to win the 1954 Sidecar TT. (Keig)

Trailing a foot on wet roads, Ray Amm races ahead of more cautious pursuers in the notorious 1954 Senior TT. He won from Geoff Duke's Gilera in an abruptly shortened race. (Keig)

Chapter 11:

Italian Domination 1955–61

1955–56

Two years with Gilera brought Geoff Duke two World Championships, but no success in the TT. In 1955 his luck changed and he showed the best of his style and brilliance to win the Senior TT convincingly, unchallenged from start to finish. Conditions were perfect, and having exceeded 97 mph in practice, it was hoped that Duke would achieve a 100 mph lap during the race. On his third lap Duke lapped in 22 min 39 sec and this was joyfully, but incorrectly, announced as a 100 mph lap record. When the correction to 99.97 mph was made over the loudspeakers spectators booed and shouted in disappointment. All this fuss about two seconds overshadowed a very fine win at 97.93 mph. Armstrong on another Gilera was second and Kavanagh third on a 500cc Guzzi single.

A very close race in the Junior almost led to the first TT win by a private owner. Bob McIntyre, a late developer, rode a Norton tuned and fully streamlined by his entrant, Joe Potts of Glasgow. The Norton and AJS racing departments had closed their eyes to streamlining in spite of Norton's pioneering work with 'kneeler' solo and sidecar motorcycles, and Potts's enterprise and McIntyre's skill put their private Norton in the lead for four out of seven Junior laps. Bob was closely harried by John Surtees (Norton) and Cecil Sandford (Guzzi), but it was the works Guzzi of Bill Lomas that worked its way through the field to pass McIntyre on the fifth lap and win by a minute. Lomas had been recruited by Guzzi at the last minute, and had to use the first three laps to 'learn' his machine. He stayed on with Guzzi and won the 1955 350cc World Championship for them.

In the 125cc TT Ubbiali confirmed his mastery of the 'tiddlers' class, winning on an MV Agusta single that carried the most complete and attractive streamlining of the 'dustbin' era. Another MV ridden by Bill Lomas won the 250cc race, run this year on the Clypse circuit. NSU were only represented by a semi-private rider, H. P. Müller, on a production racing 250cc single, for the high cost of racing and the deaths of both Hollaus and Haas led NSU to withdraw from full-time racing in 1955.

Eric Oliver, now a veteran of 20 years of solo and sidecar racing, fought a gritty battle to keep up with three much faster BMW works outfits. A wheel-to-wheel contest with Schneider ended when Oliver's passenger's eye was damaged by smashed goggles, and Noll succeeded in wiping a cylinder off his BMW when he miscalculated a bend. Schneider won.

1956

In 1956 John Surtees took the Senior TT on a factory MV Agusta, quickly building up a lead of a minute ahead of Lomas's factory Guzzi. Lomas finished second, followed by two works Nortons and Walter Zeller from Germany on the lone works BMW. Surtees was not a happy young man before this race, for inept pit work had lost him the Junior TT, and he was riding a well-worn practice machine in the Senior. A collision with a straying cow in practice damaged the motorcycle built specially for the TT by MV, demonstrating that errant livestock were still a hazard on the Isle of Man.

It was a case of survival of the mechanically fittest in the 1956 Junior, as one leader after another retired. Bill Lomas, still on top form in the last of six distinguished years of TT competition, retired while leading, Surtees ran out of fuel and Kavanagh (Guzzi) won.

Ubbiali won the 125 and 250cc classes by large margins in two uninspiring races, but the rather poor reputation of the Clypse circuit was saved for another year at least by a splendid battle in the sidecar race between members of the BMW team, which left one survivor, Hillebrand, to win.

A move back to the mountain from the Clypse did not save the Clubman's TT from extinction in 1957. Since 1953 it had become a BSA Gold Star benefit, to the confusion of those who thought that one needed overhead camshafts to go fast.

The glitter of the second Golden Age had lost some of its sheen. Some great riders had died in accidents between 1951 and 1955. The governing organization of international racing, the FIM (Fédération Internationale Motorcycliste), was going through a particularly dictatorial phase and doing its best to make life difficult for riders and entrants. Finally, throughout Europe and the UK, profits from motorcycle sales were falling. The outlook was not a happy one at the end of 1956.

1957

> 'Previous experience of British bikes didn't count for very much when it came to taking a Gilera down Bray Hill, past the Highlander, through Glen Helen . . . and up and down Snaefell' – *Bob McIntyre on 1957 TT practice.*

The 50th anniversary of the TT races was marked by extending the Senior to eight laps, and by two wins that firmly established Bob McIntyre as one of the very greatest TT riders. McIntyre had two terrible seasons with AJS after winning the 1952 Manx Grand Prix, and chose to stay with his private entrant, Joe Potts, in 1955 and 1956, winning many national races, and rejecting offers from MV, Moto Guzzi and Gilera. Late in 1956 he joined Gilera, however, replacing Bob Armstrong, who had decided to retire.

The weather was glorious; Rem Fowler and Jack Marshall were present to recall how much harder it had been back in 1907 and Stanley Woods forgot his age and borrowed a works Guzzi in practice to lap at 82 mph. Gilera, MV and Guzzi built completely new machines for the Senior and Junior races, Gilera entering the 350cc class for the first time and that wonderful box of tricks, the V-eight Moto Guzzi, was brought across to the Isle of Man for Dickie Dale to ride. Norton and AJS no longer entered works teams; Joe Craig had died in a road accident in March of 1957 and 33 years' association with Norton and the TT ended.

McIntyre led the first lap of the Junior race, but was passed (on time) by Dale on the single-cylinder Guzzi and Hartle on a works-tuned Norton entered by Eric Bowers. Hartle gained on Dale, but on lap 4 oil on the road at Quarry Bends threw off both riders, injuring Hartle and damaging Dale's Guzzi. Bob McIntyre retook the lead, the misfire that slowed him down after his first lap was cured at a pit stop, and he won from Keith Campbell (Guzzi) and Bob Brown (Gilera).

The Lightweight classes provided two exciting races, a novelty for Clypse solo races. In a Mondial-MV battle Provini worked through the field after a bad start on his Mondial in the 125cc class. Ubbiali tried to keep up on his MV, passing Miller and Taveri, but could only finish second. Sammy Miller and Cecil Sandford disputed the lead in the 250cc class on their Mondials until Miller fell off at Governor's Bridge, just after passing Sandford, which let Taveri (MV) and Colombo (MV) into second and third places. Tito Provini broke the Clypse lap record at 78 mph before retiring, having shown himself to be a stylish and very aggressive rider.

An air of anticipation, bright sunny weather and a fine international entry on Europe's fastest motorcycles all contributed to a wonderful atmosphere for the Jubilee Senior TT. Geoff Duke and Bob Armstrong took a leaf from Stanley Wood's book to keep McIntyre well informed from a signalling station at Sulby. McIntyre at No 72 was one of the last to start and it was soon clear that he did not plan a waiting game. His first lap broke Duke's 1955 record, at 99.99 mph, and on four laps he exceeded the magic 100 mph, setting the new record of 101.12 mph on his fourth lap. John Surtees held second place throughout the race, and Walter Zeller (BMW) held a superb third until his ignition failed, on a machine noted for reliability rather than speed.

McIntyre handled his Gilera as if it was a lightweight, and on lap 5 his distinguished signallers at Sulby urged him to ease off. He completed the eight laps in a little under two hours 40 minutes, at an average of 99.4 mph, followed by Surtees (MV), Brown (Gilera) and Campbell (Guzzi).

It was a resounding Jubilee series, the last in which Guzzi and Gilera competed as factory entrants. At the end of the 1957 season they and Mondial announced their withdrawal from racing: DKW, NSU, Norton and AJS had already closed their racing departments, leaving MV Agusta, BMW and Morini as the only significant European factories to keep on competing.

In a way, the decision of Signor Agusta to

continue to support international racing did not help competition between 1958 and 1960. Every 500cc World Championship race except the 1960 Ulster GP and every single 350cc Championship race between 1958 and 1960 was won by an MV. In the same period every solo TT race, irrespective of class (except the 1959 Formula 1 races), was won by an MV from the Gallarati racing department. No private or small firm could hope to match the experience and resources of MV Agusta.

Having said this, there were interesting developments during these years; in 1958 Mike Hailwood entered four TT events, finishing in all of them and achieving third place in the 250cc class on an NSU. John Surtees won the Senior and Junior TT races.

In 1959 the East German MZ organization entered the Lightweight 125cc and 250cc races, with Taveri, Fugner and development engineer Degner as riders. The Japanese Honda factory also entered both lightweight classes with machines that used a number of suspension and engine design features of the 1954 NSU twins. Both firms were to build on their first experiences. John Surtees won a stormy Senior TT and a record Junior. This was the last year the Clypse Course was used and the Lightweight races were returned to the Mountain Course for 1960. Geoff Duke took fourth place in the 1959 Senior TT, his last Isle of Man race and the end of a brilliant racing career. Duke's international successes in early 1950s stimulated wide public interest in motorcycling and in the TT itself. After retiring as a rider he continued, and continues now, to serve motorcycle racing as an entrant, team manager and public relations man.

1960

Honda and MZ returned to the Isle of Man with much improved 125cc and 250cc machines, and much stronger teams of riders. Honda's 250 four-cylinder machine was not yet fast enough to beat the fastest MV and Morini singles, but it was reliable, Bob Brown taking fourth place in front of two Japanese Honda team-mates. Both 125cc and 250cc races were incredibly fast, Carlo Ubbiali winning the 125cc race at 86.13 mph and Gary Hocking the 250cc race at 93.64 mph, both on MV Agustas.

John Surtees lapped at 99.2 mph in the Junior race, but gearbox and valve gear problems slowed him to second place behind John Hartle on the second works MV. Bob McIntyre raced hard and consistently to hold third place until the finish, to average over 95 mph on his AJS single.

The return to the Mountain Course of sidecar racing was only moderately successful. A small field, bad weather and numerous breakdowns deprived spectators of close racing over the long course. Larger fields were to provide exciting sidecar racing over the Mountain later, but not in 1960. Helmuth Fath (BMW) won from Pip Harris (BMW), establishing a new lap record of 85.82 mph, which was over 27 mph faster than the previous record set in 1925 by Freddie Dixon.

Nothing went wrong for Surtees in the 1960 Senior TT, another very fast race. He stayed well in front of Hartle's MV, averaged over 103 mph for the six laps and set a new lap record at 104.08 mph. Derek Minter and Mike Hailwood achieved the first over-100 mph laps on British machines, Nortons in both cases, and Hailwood went on to finish third behind the MVs, while Minter retired. Hailwood had become a major rider in three seasons of TT racing. His flippant, relaxed manner did not compare well with Surtees's serious, business-like approach, but Hailwood's ability and courage soon earned him the respect he deserved.

1961

> 'You go up Snaefell on the machine and down on your nerves' – *Bob McIntyre.*

John Surtees retired from motorcycle racing after the 1960 season, having won six TTs out of 14 starts, with only one retirement, and six World Championship titles. MV Agusta announced that they would not enter the TT officially, but that they would lend 'private' rider Gary Hocking a 500cc machine – plus a 350cc, a 250cc and 125cc – and a few mechanics.

Hocking, a Welsh-born Rhodesian, had no luck with his stable of MVs. In the Junior TT he could not get clear of Mike Hailwood (AJS), who started immediately after him, and he over-revved the MV, damaging the valves and pistons. On the last lap Hailwood's gudgeon pin collapsed, and the Junior went to young Phil Read in his first TT, Hocking finished second and set a new lap record of 99.80 mph.

In the Senior Mike Hailwood gave determined chase again and Hocking again over-revved and this time had to retire. Hailwood's Norton engine was built and tuned by Bill Lacey, an ex-Brooklands racer, and Mike averaged 100 mph to win from Bob McIntyre on another Norton single. Third was the

'Domiracer' Norton twin produced by Norton's development engineer Doug Hele, and ridden by Australian Tom Phillis.

Mike Hailwood and Gary Hocking started the Lightweight TT together, and fought a nose-to-tail battle until the MV retired after lap 2. Hocking was a brilliant rider who believed himself unbeatable, and after the TT fiasco he went on to win nine Grands Prix to become 1961 World Champion in both the 350cc and 500cc classes. But Bob McIntyre was the sensation of the Lightweight TT. He went straight in the lead with a lap at over 99 mph, then broke the 1960 Junior lap record, and drew ahead, in a class of his own, until his engine seized on the last lap, leaving Hailwood to win. Poor McIntyre was surely the unluckiest top flight rider of his time, but at least no ill luck had robbed him of his 1957 'Golden' wins.

Honda took the first five places in the 250cc race, and the first six in the 125cc TT, Mike Hailwood winning both races. Max Deubel (BMW) won the sidecar TT from Fritz Scheidegger (BMW) in a race marred by the death of sidecar passenger Marie Lambert in a crash just after Crag-ny-Baa. Deubel's fastest lap was 87.97 mph.

1962

Honda ventured into the heftier classes in 1962, with a bored-out version of the 250cc four. It was not sorted out in time for the TT, so Hocking, now joined by Hailwood in the MV Agusta team, was favourite for both Junior and Senior races. In the Junior, Gary went ahead, but Mike made fastest lap of the race (101.58 mph) on the second lap, and slowly wore down Hocking's lead. Both MV's ran rough on the last lap, and perhaps Mike had a little more power to pull him in front to win by only 5½ seconds. There were two fatal crashes; in one of them Tom Phillis was killed at Laurel Bank, possibly trying too hard to keep up with the two MV Agustas on his Junior Honda.

In the Senior, Hocking left Mike behind, setting a new lap record of 105.75 mph, and increasing his lead. When Hailwood's clutch began to fail, Mike had to retire and Phil Read (Norton) finished second.

A 50cc TT race was introduced in 1961. Here at last were the 'freaks' to end all freaks. These tiny bikes with tiny riders exceeded 70 mph around the Mountain circuit on narrow tyres, keeping their motors spinning at over 10,000 revs by continuous footwork on 12-speed gearboxes. The winner was Ernst Degner, who had defected from East Germany in 1961 to take his considerable technical experience and flair to Suzuki of Japan.

Degner's dramatic departure from the East made him particularly unpopular with MZ, for he actually defected during the 1961 Swedish GP, retiring while in the lead, and in the running for the 125cc World Championship. Supposedly he also took the secrets of MZ's inspired designer Walter Kaaden as well, and so paved the way for Japanese two-stroke supremacy from the later 1960s on.

In 1962 four-strokes still set the pace in the Lightweight classes, and Honda dominated the 125 and 250cc classes. Bob McIntyre again exceeded 99 mph before retiring in the Lightweight on a Honda. Derek Minter won the 250cc race and Luigi Taveri the 125cc race.

Mishaps and broken engines removed Chris Vincent's BMW opposition in the sidecar race and he won a popular victory on his BSA twin outfit; Max Deubel retired on the last lap, four minutes in the lead after lapping at 90.7 mph on his first lap.

The fastest rider on the Island in 1955 on the fastest machine. Geoff Duke won the Senior TT convincingly on the works Gilera, touching down here at Ballaugh Bridge. (EMAP)

Full streamlining reached its peak of development in 1957. Ubbiali keeps ahead of Taveri, both on MVs. Full streamlining was banned after the 1957 season. (Keig)

Another of Italy's great riders, Tarquino Provini, winning the 1957 125cc TT on an FB Mondial. (Keig)

Master of the 1957 Senior TT, Bob McIntyre made full use of the Gilera's power to set new lap and race records. He had never raced the Gilera before. (Keig)

Previous experience of British bikes did not count for much when it came to taking a Gilera down Bray Hill. Bob McIntyre is approaching the Gilera's maximum of 160 mph at this point. **(Island Photographics)**

Australian Keith Campbell at speed on the Guzzi single which he rode to fifth place in the 1957 Senior TT. Moto Guzzi used their own wind tunnel from 1951 to lead the development of low drag designs. **(Keig)**

Walter Zeller helped to develop the works BMWs as well as race them. He was fourth in 1956, but retired in 1957, the year he is seen here. **(Keig)**

Geoff Duke was 35 when he raced this BMW in the 1958 Senior TT and retired. His brilliant racing career should have been longer, but for a run of bad luck in his last years with Gilera, followed by failure to find the right machine. **(Keig)**

Mike Hailwood was 13th in his first Senior TT on a Norton. He was also third in the 250cc race. **(Keig)**

Below: *By 1958 BMWs were unbeatable in sidecar racing. Helmut Fath retired in 1958 on the Clypse Circuit, seen here, but won the 1960 race on the Mountain Circuit.* **(Keig)**

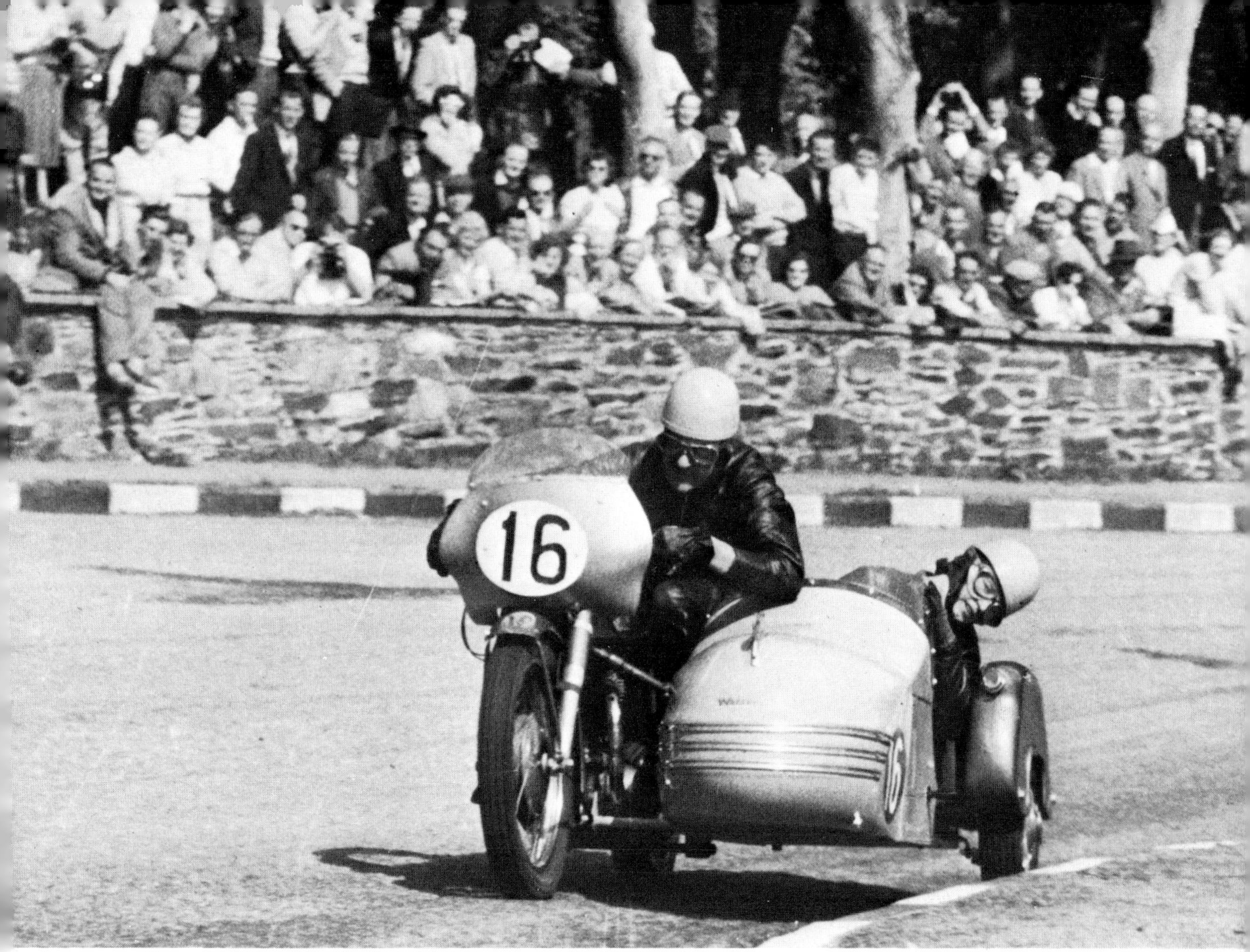

Above: *Eric Oliver raced a standard Norton twin and touring sidecar in the 1958 TT, passengered by Pat Wise, and came tenth. She said she enjoyed every minute of it!* **(Keig)**

The first Hondas to race in Europe in 1959 were 125cc twins with several NSU-like features. N. Taniguchu took Honda's first ever place (sixth) in a TT. **(Keig)**

The Senior TT was one of the few Championship races that Gary Hocking did not win in 1961. In trying to lose Mike Hailwood he over-revved the MV and had to retire with a damaged engine. **(Keig)**

Below: *Hailwood presses on to his first International TT win, the 1961 Senior. His unexpected defeat of Hocking gave Norton their last 500cc TT win.* **(Keig)**

Flat out at the bottom of Bray Hill, Tom Phillis rode this Norton 'Domiracer' twin to a fine third place behind Hailwood and McIntyre in the 1961 Senior TT. (EMAP)

Riding a works Honda four, Bob McIntyre lapped at just under 100 mph to set a new Lightweight lap record in 1961. He retired, but later won the Ulster Grand Prix, where he is seen in his characteristic crouch. (EMAP)

Chapter 12:

Japanese Takeover 1962–67

1963

> 'I never underestimated Hartle, I knew he would give me a hard time, especially in the TT' – *Mike Hailwood.*

Suzuki, Yamaha, Honda, Tohatsu: Japanese technology and Japanese resources were beginning to swamp the Lightweight classes. And Japanese development of German induction science changed the two-stroke from a little plodder to a little screamer, capable of 90 mph from 50cc.

In the 125cc race, the winning Suzuki lapped at 91.32 mph, while the best Honda could manage was fourth place. In the 250cc race Jim Redman (Honda) only beat Fumio Ito (Yamaha) because the superb Japanese rider made a very leisurely pit stop, and Mitsuo Itoh won the 50cc race on another two-stroke Suzuki. Honda had their 350cc four in Championship-winning shape in 1963, and Mike Hailwood (MV) could only watch Jim Redman pull away in the Junior TT before Mike dropped out and John Hartle took over second place on one of the Geoff Duke Gileras. This was one of three 350cc and two 500cc fours taken out of retirement at Geoff Duke's insistent suggestion, and raced as a team, with Derek Minter and John Hartle as riders and Geoff as team manager. The six-year-old machines were meticulously rebuilt, with help from the Ferrari car racing organization, by Fumagalli, the Gilera mechanic who also tended the machines, and in the 500cc class at least, they made a strong challenge to Mike Hailwood.

In the Senior TT John Hartle started ten seconds before Hailwood, and used all the road, and a little more, to keep in front for the first lap. He lapped at over 105 mph and looked the fastest man in the race, but Hailwood lapped at over 106 mph, and on the second lap, after following Hartle closely for several miles, passed him and drew ahead to win by a little over 1½ minutes from the Gilera. Phil Read, who had taken over Minter's place in 'Scuderia Duke' after Minter crashed badly at Brands Hatch, was third. Swiss drivers Florian Camathias and Fritz Scheidegger were first and second in the Sidecar race, both on BMWs, though Camathias called his an FCS as he was not on good terms with BMW. In general, the early 1960s seemed a time for inter-team disharmony. In the Honda team Jim Redman was 'head boy' and was less than charming to more recent team members. Gary Hocking was 'bought' out of the MZ team by MV Agusta, whose machines he then ran down, while Carlo Ubbiali was also something of a *prima donna*. The Japanese factories hired and fired riders without second thoughts, and their remoteness from the European racing arena led them to make some unreasonable demands on their riders. Bob McIntyre was not at the 1963 TT, for he had crashed fatally at Oulton Park late in 1962. A combination of hard riding and bad luck led to his retirement in seven out of his last ten TTs, to the disappointment of his friends and fans, who included many riders whom he had quietly and freely helped with advice and encouragement.

1964–66

> 'In the light of their [Honda's] history of atrocious handling, Jim Redman comes out as a far better rider than most people are prepared to give him credit for' – *Mike Hailwood.*

The 'heavyweight' TT races of 1964 and 1965 gave MV and Mike Hailwood two 500cc wins, and Jim Redman two 350cc wins. In 1964 both won relatively easily. In 1965, in wet and foul conditions, Hailwood fell off at Sarah's Cottage and some blacksmith mechanicking at the pits was needed to repair his Senior MV enough to continue. Then a bad misfire cut his speed and Mike stopped again to remove a plug and continue more smoothly on three cylinders and win.

MV produced a new three-cylinder '350' for the 1965 Junior race, on which Hailwood caught Jim Redman and led until he retired. Giacomo Agostini joined MV for 1965 and finished third in his first TT, the 1965 Junior. A superb rider, Agostini came to the Isle of Man as an unknown Italian, but his enthusiasm and eagerness to learn English made him many new friends and admirers.

Jim Redman won the 1963, 1964 and 1965 250cc TTs, a class that Honda was determined to dominate. In 1963 Honda only just won the 250 World Championship from the amazing Italian Morini 'single' ridden by Provini. In 1964 Yamaha defeated Honda, with Phil Read taking the World Championship. Honda added money, colossal amounts of it, and cylinders, to their racing programme, and fielded a brand new six-cylinder 250cc motorcycle for 1965. Redman won the Lightweight TT on it, but only after Read had set the first over-100 mph lap and retired. There were 51 retirements out of 76 starters, and two-stroke seizure was so commonplace that riders habitually held two fingers on the clutch lever, ready for the engine stoppage that was more probable than possible.

1965

Running in second place for part of the Lightweight, in his first works ride for the Yamaha factory, was Bill Ivy, the overgrown urchin from Kent. He rode with a style and courage that brought him great success later, but in this race he frightened himself and several onlookers, and fell off when he took the wrong line at Brandywell. Bill Ivy was one of the first top-class riders to shift his weight off the saddle at corners rather than maintain the classic, smooth style of Geoff Duke and Phil Read. Not that Ivy had much weight to shift, as he was both short and slight.

1966

Mike Hailwood rejoined the Honda organization before the end of 1965, leaving Count Domenico Agusta to nurture his new favourite, Agostini. When Jim Redman withdrew from racing in 1966, these two very friendly rivals made the running in the 350 and 500cc classes, and no other rider could hold them.

Agostini won the Junior TT in commanding style, ignoring pit signals to slow after Hailwood's first-lap breakdown. Instead, the Italian increased speed to establish a new lap record of 103.09 mph. Agostini won from Peter Williams by ten full minutes, though Williams rode a very fast and consistent race on an AJS, about 20 mph slower than the MV. Mike Hailwood left Agostini three minutes behind in the Senior, and lifted the lap record to 107.07 mph.

Mike also won the 250cc race by more than five minutes from Stuart Graham, son of Les Graham, both riding six-cylinder factory Hondas. These motorcycles were easier to ride and not much slower than the 350cc fours, and Hailwood swung his Honda around the circuit at 104.29 mph – faster than his 350cc record. Neither of the works Yamahas finished.

Honda created a five-cylinder 125 at the end of 1965, a machine of unusual complexity and performance, developing around 30 bhp at 18,000 rpm. It refused to behave in the 1966 TT, and Hailwood, Bryans and Taveri could only manage sixth, seventh and eighth. Bill Ivy made full use of a healthy Yamaha twin to win the race by 30 seconds from Phil Read, hitting the roadside at least twice and lapping at 98.55 mph – on a 125.

This year the sidecar racing was close, old rivals Scheidegger and Deubel finishing within 0.8 seconds of one another. Scheidegger was disqualified for using the wrong fuel, a ridiculous technicality that was reversed months later.

The gap between factory racing machines and private owners was never greater than in the mid-60s. The main Japanese manufacturers, Yamaha and Honda especially, equated success with sales, and their development funds seemed limitless. The Honda five was only used for a year before being dropped and Yamaha and Suzuki experimented with disc and reed valves, fours and twins, all staggeringly expensive. Even in the 50cc class no expense was spared: water cooling, disc valves and double gearboxes gave these toy-like machines a top speed in excess of 100 mph – as long as the rider weighed less than eight stone!

Behind the Japanese factory bikes and the MV Agustas – usually a long way behind – machines entered by smaller factories, Bianchi, Benelli, Aermacchi and Jawa competed with the best private owners, many from Australia and southern Africa, on Nortons and Matchlesses.

1967

> 'Honda seemed quite content to leave it all to me...it was a good economic proposition for them – they were getting three men's work for one man's pay' – *Mike Hailwood.*

The Japanese assault on international racing reached a peak in 1967. Mike Hailwood was again contracted to Honda to ride in the 250cc, 350cc and 500cc classes, which committed him to a gruelling programme on powerful, ill-handling machines. Mike had raced in 30 TTs since 1958 and in 1967 he was thinking of quitting motorcycle racing. Agostini, by contrast, was only in his fourth year of international racing, on machines whose power and road-holding were finely balanced, and he was full of optimism.

The TT celebrated its Diamond Jubilee with speeches, parades and a pigeon race. The weather was fine for all races, as it had been ten years before for the Golden Jubilee. The latest Honda and Yamaha 250s achieved tremendous speeds in practice: Bill Ivy's Yamaha was timed at 152 mph on the Sulby straight, but Hailwood lapped at 105 mph, almost five mph faster than the lap record on the six-cylinder Honda, which had a top speed at least ten mph slower than the Yamaha. In the Lightweight TT Mike pulled away from the Yamahas of Read and Ivy to win at 103.07 mph.

On a 297cc Honda six, Mike won the Junior TT, opening with the fastest lap ever ridden on the Isle of Man, and using all his skill and the Honda's power to leave everyone else floundering in his wake. Agostini rode fast and competently, and was the only other finisher to average over 100 mph for the race.

Bill Ivy failed to complete a lap in the 125cc TT, in which he was favourite. Unexpectedly, Stuart Graham took the lead on a Suzuki, riding magnificently, then lost and regained it in a close race with Phil Read. Graham had the disadvantage of starting 40 seconds before Read, and Phil made a last-ditch effort to get ahead of Graham on the last lap, and succeeded by 3.4 seconds. Stuart was perhaps unlucky to lose the closest race on the Island in 1967. He then won the silliest TT ever run – the Diamond Jubilee 50cc race. The Suzuki riders Graham and Anscheidt were told that Yoshiwa Katayama (an excellent rider) was to win this race, to give Suzuki an all-Japanese win. Such team tactics have often led to farce or ill-feelings (as in the 1952 Lightweight); in 1967, it was farce. Katayama made a poor start, so Anscheidt and Graham pottered round until he caught up with them. Then Katayama fell off while trying to spot an oil leak on Anscheidt's machine as he rode alongside, and could not restart. Graham won.

The Senior TT of 1967 ranks with the 1935 Senior as one of the greatest motorcycle races ever. Agostini lapped faster than Hailwood in practice, depriving Mike of the psychological advantage he usually had at the start. Then, starting 30 seconds after Mike, Agostini rode a blistering opening lap at a new record of 108.77 mph. Starting his second lap over ten seconds behind, Mike re-took the lap record, riding with equal ferocity to Agostini and closed the gap to two seconds when both riders stopped for fuel after the third lap. It was obvious that Hailwood had a serious problem as he and his mechanics tried and failed to secure a loose twistgrip which was coming off the handlebars as the Honda pitched round the circuit. After wasting ten seconds hammering the end of the handlebar, Hailwood set off to make up the enlarged deficit. Both men rode at their limit, touching the verges and skimming stone walls, but both placed their motorcycles exactly and showed that style can be part of fast riding. In spite of his problems, Hailwood closed up to within one second of Agostini on the fourth lap, then actually led by one second at Ramsey on the fifth. Agostini retook the lead up the Mountain road – then lost his chain and damaged the rear-wheel sprocket, and was out. Hailwood cruised to the finish, nearly eight minutes ahead of Peter Williams on an Arter-Matchless and Steve Spencer on a Lancefield Norton.

Agostini had almost won on the day of his 25th birthday. He went on to beat Mike Hailwood in the Belgian and Italian Grands Prix and won the World Championship in the 500cc class. Mike, 27 years old, seemed much older than Agostini, and had laboured hard and dangerously to give Honda a fistful of World Championships. In 1967 he took the 250cc and 350cc titles, but imperfect preparation of his 'four' eliminated him from the Italian GP and lost him his chance of the 500cc title.

By the end of 1967 the 500cc Honda not only still handled atrociously, it was only a few mph faster than the bigger MV 'three', and Mike determined not to renew his contract unless Honda built a good frame for their '500'. But Honda were now interested in car racing and dropped out of Motorcycle Grands Prix, paying Hailwood a handsome fee to stay out of World Championship events in 1968. Honda and Hailwood left the TT and it was to be many years before both came back to race on the Isle of Man.

Jim Redman led the Honda team in 1963. His win in the Lightweight TT helped towards his World Championship in the 250cc class that year. **(Keig)**

Fumio Ito rode like a demon on a works Yamaha twin to lead the 1963 Lightweight TT until slowed by a leisurely pitstop. **(Keig)**

John Hartle did his damnedest to keep ahead of Mike Hailwood in the 1963 Senior, riding close to the limit of adhesion on his Duke-entered Gilera. **(Keig)**

Mike Hailwood pulled past Hartle at the end of lap 1 and gradually drew away from him on the works MV. **(Keig)**

Phil Read did not keep up with the two leaders on his Duke Gilera, but still averaged over 100 mbh to finish third. (Keig)

Florian Camathias drives out of Quarter Bridge on his way to win the 1963 Sidecar TT. (Keig)

Second place in 1963 went to another Swiss, Fritz Scheidegger. **(BMW)**

Max Deubel won the 1964 Sidecar TT. He also won in 1961 and 1965, on a BMW each time. **(Keig)**

Jim Redman won the Junior and 250cc TT races in 1963, but only managed eighth place in the 125cc race. He is seen at Parliament Square, Ramsey. (Mike Corrin)

Ernst Degner took third place in the 1963 125cc race on the Suzuki he had helped to develop. It was virtually a copy of the 1962 East German MZ. (Mike Corrin)

Mike Hailwood won several of his TTs in dramatic circumstances. In 1965 he crashed in the wet at Sarah's Cottage, but repaired his MV enough to carry on and win. The shattered screen and flattened exhaust can be seen in this picture. **(Mike Corrin)**

Bill Ivy's exciting riding brought him several lap records and two TT wins. This 1966 125cc TT shot shows his typical bent-arm style, as he heads for the first of his wins. **(Mike Corrin)**

1967, Hailwood's last year as Honda works rider. On his favourite machine, the 297cc six-cylinder, he broke the absolute lap record during the Junior TT. **(EMAP)**

Below: *As Agostini whams the bottom of Bray Hill at over 140 mph, his suspension bottoms and he is thrown off the saddle. This was during his tremendous battle with Hailwood for the lead in the 1967 Senior TT.* **(EMAP)**

Stuart Graham had a short, successful career as a motorcycle racer before turning to car racing. Like his father Les Graham, he was a stylish rider. He was second in the 1966 250cc TT on this factory Honda 'six'. **(EMAP)**

Below: *Benelli returned to the Isle of Man in 1967 with new 350cc and 500cc four-cylinder machines. Renzo Pasolini was the rider and in 1968 he took second place in both Junior and Lightweight races.* **(Mike Corrin)**

Chapter 13:

Too Many Races 1968–80

From 281 riders entered in five races to 508 riders entered in ten races. Perhaps the biggest change in the TT between 1957 and 1968 was sheer numbers. There were certainly as many skilled and courageous riders on the Isle of Man in 1968 as in 1957, but with so many races the drama was inevitably less concentrated.

By 1980 entries were up to 600, and the TT had developed from part of the International World Championship race programme into an independent motorcycling festival. As true road-racing steadily disappeared from the Continent and even the Nurburgring was discarded as too dangerous, the TT was excluded from the World Championships. Free to alter and add races at will, the ACU changed the TT programme to provide what it believed would give spectators the best entertainment. A generation of specialist TT riders who had little interest in overseas racing emerged.

There were some great races in this period and some very successful additions to the programme, such as the so-called Classic 1000cc TT. But it would be impossible to describe every race – and I have tried to choose some of the most exciting.

1968

Giacomo Agostini won every Senior TT between 1968 and 1973, inclusive, and every Junior TT except the 1971 race. No other motorcycle could challenge the speed, stability and reliability of the factory MV Agustas and Agostini rode superbly and intelligently. During this period he won the 350cc and 500cc World Championships every year and in 1968 he won every single major 350cc and 500cc International Grand Prix, as John Surtees had done in 1959.

Agostini never had to ride as fast as he did in 1967, and never equalled the lap speed of 108.38 mph he achieved in his great battle with Mike Hailwood. Far behind him were some fierce races, such as Alan Bennett's wheel-to-wheel battle with Peter Williams in 1970. Bennett (Seeley) starting No. 3, caught up with Williams (Arter Matchless) starting No. 5, but Williams fought back and the pair averaged over 100 mph on their 500cc singles until Bennett crashed at Doran's bend. Williams finished second to Agostini.

In 1968 the main drama was rivalry and ill-feeling within the Yamaha team. Although Phil Read had ridden and helped develop the Yamaha since 1964, Yamaha decided that Bill Ivy would be their star rider in 1968, after he won the 1967 125cc World Championship. Understandably Read was furious at this policy and the crass way that it was announced, and told Ivy that he would not make it easy for him.

Bill Ivy took off like the well-known scalded cat in the 250cc TT, breaking the lap record from a standing start (105.81 mph), then nearly broke his foot when he trapped it under the gear-lever. In considerable pain he continued, Phil Read going into the lead on the second works Yamaha. Then Read's rear tyre punctured and Bill Ivy won the race and was lifted off his machine for medical attention.

Ivy also made the fastest lap in the 125cc race – a memorable 100.32 mph. However, this was to be Phil Read's race, by order of Yamaha management, and Bill stopped at Creg-ny-Baa to make certain that Read won. Relations between Read and Ivy got steadily worse throughout 1968 until both riders were ready to sabotage a win by the other by fair means or foul. Read won both 125 and 250cc Championships from an unlucky and thoroughly bitter Ivy, and Yamaha disbanded its factory team after 1968.

In Yamaha's absence in 1969, the Australian Kel Carruthers won the Lightweight on a four-cylinder Benelli, then Yamaha came back in 1970 and won every 250cc TT between 1970 and 1980. Carruthers won in 1970, then Phil Read, Chas Mortimer, Charlie Williams and Tom Herron shared ten 250cc TTs between them, Williams taking five of them. The post-1969 Yamahas were twin-cylinder machines, sold also in less developed form to private owners, and the Yamaha became the 'boy racer' of the 1970s. Bill Ivy's 1968 lap record stood until 1979, when Charlie Williams broke it with 106.03 mph. The 125cc lap record was never broken, for this class disappeared from the programme in 1975.

Formula 750

Probably the most successful addition to the TT races was the Formula 750, introduced in 1971. This class opened the TT to the superbikes of the 1970s, modified and rebuilt to challenge the speed of full Grand Prix 500cc machines, and it produced some of the best racing on the Isle of Man. In 1972 Peter Williams's Formula 750 Norton, a full racing push-rod Commando 750, was timed at 146.9 mph on the Highlander speed trap in a year that Agostini's Senior MV was clocked at 154.5 mph.

Formula 750 and its successor, the Classic 1000cc TT, helped to lift the TT out of the abyss into which it was sinking in the early 1970s. A combination of too many races and the monotonous victories of Agostini and MV Agusta had killed off much of the excitement of the taut programme of earlier years, as well as ensuring that the prize money for non-factory entrants (over 99 percent of riders in 1972) was too thinly spread. The death of Gilberto Parlotti on the Mountain road while leading a rain soaked 125cc TT in 1972 made Agostini, a close friend, quit the TT and devote himself to an anti-TT campaign. Arguments raged over the quality of the Island roads, the competence of marshals and the safety of racing motorcycles.

Matters were not helped by the decline of the European motorcycle industry. Even the best-prepared Norton and AJS singles were much slower than over-bored Yamahas in 1972, and the Patons, Aermacchis, Jawas and Benellis that had added technical interest were absent. In 1974 the Senior, Junior, 250cc, 125cc and 500cc sidecar races were all won by Yamahas, which some people felt was an overdose of Japanese two-strokes.

So Formula 750 allowed British Triumph and BSA triples and Norton Commandos to race, and beat, the two-strokes. The 1971 and 1972 races were won by Alan Jeffries and Roy Pickrell on Triumphs at well over 100 mph. In 1973 it seemed that Jack Findley might thrust his Suzuki triple in front of the British machines, for he was a determined and experienced rider on a very fast motorcycle. Findley was defeated by the enormous thirst of his Suzuki, which needed two stops for fuel, and by the magnificent riding of Peter Williams on a John Player Special Norton, developed and largely built by himself. Williams is a gifted and inventive engineer and his controversial ideas about magnesium wheels, monocoque frames and disc brakes all became common practice later on.

In the 1973 Formula 750 race, run in fine weather, Williams tucked himself inside his Norton to lead from start to finish and win at an average of 105.47 mph, a race speed exceeded only by the Agostini-Hailwood battle of 1967. Behind him Findley fought off Alan Jeffries's Triumph triple. At a time when riders were hanging farther and farther off their machines, Williams sat firmly in the saddle and managed to ride very fast while looking almost slow.

Jack Findley won the 1973 Senior on a Suzuki twin from Peter Williams, now on an Arter-Matchless single. Williams recorded the fastest lap ever on a single-cylinder machine at 102.74 mph, and received just £350 prize money for his second place. Small wonder that few continental riders now come to the Isle of Man.

It could not last, and Japanese machines took over Formula 750 and its successor, the 1000cc and Open Classic races. By 1976 even the Production TT races were lost to foreign machines, and 'Slippery Sam', the Trident that seemed to have as tough and positive a character as its many riders, had won its last victory. That was the four-hour long Production 1000cc TT in 1974, when its riders were Dave Croxford, a cheerful, extrovert Londoner, and Alex George, a quiet Scot whose riding suggested he was born without fear.

The Classic TT

The Classic TT took over from the Senior TT as the climax of TT week. Mick Grant had made several very fast laps since his first TT in 1970, and in 1975 he broke Mike Hailwood's 1967 record with a lap at 109.82 mph on a 750cc Kawasaki triple. The big Kawasakis, Suzukis and the Yamaha TZ 750 produced over 100 bhp, and riders capable of using this power on the TT circuit steadily increased lap speeds on the Isle of Man. Such riders were Mick Grant, Tony Rutter and John Williams, who raised the lap record to 112.27 mph on a 500cc Suzuki in 1976.

Another group of men who mastered the Isle of Man races were riders from Ulster: Tom Herron, Joey Dunlop, Steve Cull, Rob McElnea – who started racing on Northern Irish road circuits far narrower, bumpier, and usually wetter, than the Mountain circuit. Dunlop won his first TT in 1977, the 1000cc Jubilee, with a lap at 110 mph. By 1980 Dunlop's winning speed in the Classic TT was 112.7 mph and his absolute lap record was 115.22 mph.

The Senior TT 1977–80

The spectacle of big bikes capable of 170 mph in the Classic TT reduced the Senior TT to one of many supporting races, but for a period of three years the return of two of the fastest riders of the 1960s restored some of its old glory to the 500cc race. By 1977 the ACU had a treasure chest large enough to attract Phil Read back to the race which he had earlier written off as too dangerous, and in 1978 Mike Hailwood also raced again on the circuit which had always been his favourite.

Phil Read's return was distinguished by two excellent wins: the Formula 1 TT and the Senior. For the Formula race Honda prepared one of their big, (920cc) endurance-racing four-cylinder four-strokes, which Read wrestled round to win by 38 seconds from a Ducati superbly ridden by Roger Nichols. It was a tough race for Read; deteriorating weather caused the race to be shortened to four laps, and even so Read had blistered hands from grappling the big Honda. Read had an easier win in the Senior TT. His main opponent, John Williams, retired on lap 1 and Read pulled well ahead of a close race for the next five places. Pat Hennen, a young Californian, made the greatest impact by an American rider since Jake de Rosier by finishing fifth in his first TT.

In 1978 Read was joined on the Isle of Man by Mike Hailwood, entered on a Ducati V-twin in the Formula 1 race, and on Yamahas in the 250cc and Senior races. Mike's Yamahas failed, but the Ducati ran perfectly. After Tom Herron's leading Honda began to come apart, Hailwood took the lead on time in the Formula race, and proceeded to chase Phil Read on the road. Read started No. 1, Hailwood No. 12, and on the third lap Hailwood had caught up and was tailing Read from Ramsey to the top of Snaefell. Then Hailwood went in front, and soon after their refuelling stop Read's Honda gave up. Hailwood broke the Formula 1 record by 1½ minutes and his many admirers, who had wondered how ten years' absence would affect his performance, were overjoyed.

Unhappily, it was a grim TT year otherwise. Five entrants, including three sidecar riders, were killed during the racing and the promising American Pat Hennen pushed himself too far in the Senior TT in a desperate attempt to take the lead from Tom Herron. Herron could see that Hennen was on the edge of disaster as he raced wheel to wheel with the Californian, and tried to signal him to take it easy, but as Herron pulled ahead Hennen missed his line at high speed and crashed violently, receiving injuries that ended his racing career.

The ACU pre-judged any findings from its enquiries into these fatalities with a statement that read: 'Until the investigations are complete the ACU consider that both incidents are part and parcel of any form of speed sport, and while regretting the incidents, will continue with the TT series'. This view was not shared by the FIM, nor by the newspapers that profited from misfortune to give the TT a blast of bad publicity. The ACU would have done better to withhold its opinions until after the inquiries. A lot of hot air was blown one way and another, leaving the basic problem unresolved: the TT is still more dangerous than any other international motorcycle race. This is not a reason for stopping it, but no rider, scrutineer or organizer should deceive himself that it is not so.

Hailwood rode again in 1979. This time his Ducati disgraced itself in the Formula 1 race, for gears, battery and exhaust pipes all went missing, while Alex George (Honda), on the top of his form, led from the start and broke race and lap records. The Senior was Hailwood's race, however, and on a works Suzuki that seemed to be tailored to fit, Mike broke the Senior lap record at 114.02 mph and led Alex George home. The Classic TT provided the finest match between beefed-up roadster and pure Grand Prix machine ever seen on the Isle of Man. George drove ahead and led Hailwood by nine, four, then three and a half seconds after lap 4. Then Hailwood led George by less than a second. George was signalled the situation, and using every ounce of his skill and grit lapped at 114.18 mph to beat Hailwood, 'with a heavy heart' at defeating 'Mike the Bike'.

Run almost entirely in sunny weather, the 1979 TT once more lifted the stature of the race. The contrast between powerful four-strokes and high-revving two-strokes, the contrast between Mike Hailwood and Mick Grant's smooth style and the energetic weight shifting of Ron Haslam and Steve

Tonkin, and exciting riding of Alex George, who looked both stylish and very fast – all made for one of the best years of the decade.

1980 brought back controversy about safety and speed after Alex George crashed badly in practice – medical help took a long time to arrive. Joey Dunlop set a new absolute lap record of 115.22 mph on a TZ750 Yamaha. Charlie Williams won his tenth TT to rank among the great riders on the Isle of Man – no man won as many TTs on Yamahas.

Today the lap record stands at a shade over 121 mph, set by Steve Hislop, and he and Joey Dunlop are undoubtedly masters of the Island circuit. Nortons (rotary engined) started with a chance in the Senior TT and there are hopes that the new Norton organization will thrive and continue to support racing.

Production and Sidecar TT races.

Production and Clubman's racing have hardly been mentioned in this history, not for lack of respect for the skill and speed of its participants but for lack of space. The fastest production racers today would have given Mike Hailwood and his works Honda a hard race in 1967.

So too, incredibly, would the fastest modern sidecars. Sidecar racing has become one of the main attractions of TT week since larger numbers have taken part. From 1955 to 1975, the sidecar class was dominated by German machines, BMWs, the tough shaft-drive opposed twins withstanding the treatment they received from their riders, from Friedrich Hillebrand, to Siggi Schauzu, who won nine sidecar TTs and lapped at over 99 mph in 1975. To watch sidecar outfits bounce and lurch at over 130 mph over the short, bumpy straights between Ginger Hall and Ramsey makes one wonder what sort of person would take such risks.

Sidecar racers are a different breed from solo riders – usually shorter, older and more resigned to the effects of vibration and 'G' forces on machine reliability. The days of sidecars bolted on to solo racing motorcycles have long gone, and the last BMW-powered outfits were multi-tube-framed vehicles whose driver controlled the vehicle from a kneeling position. Later Yamaha-powered outfits with aluminium box-type chassis closed the gap between the fastest sidecars and the fastest solos, and travel so fast that they leave the ground as dramatically as solos at Ballaugh Bridge and the hump on the bottom of Bray Hill, now known as Ago's leap.

Several women have competed successfully in the most recent TT races, though none took part in a solo TT before Beryl Swain in 1962. It has always been felt that the gentle sex should be protected from exposure to physical risk – particularly when they actually beat men, as Fay Taylour did in one of the very first dirt-track races in the 1920s. Nevertheless women regularly race in sidecars – a jarring and dangerous occupation – and Julia Bingham has clambered around Dennis Bingham's outfit at lap speeds well over 100 mph to help him to two TT second places. The sidecar lap record in 1980 stood at 106.08 mph, and was set by Jack Taylor, passengered by Benga Johansson.

Conclusion

'Is the game worth the Candle?'

This was the question the *Isle of Man Examiner* asked after the first TT death in 1911 and it has been asked ever since. Clearly very many riders believe that the risks are worth taking, for the number of TT entries continues to grow, but responsibility for the degree of danger is shared by riders and the organizers. As road improvements make the course smoother, riders naturally go faster, past the lamp posts and dry-stone walls. But without the lamp posts and dry-stone walls there would be no TT. Is there an answer? Just as many accidents have occurred in the smaller-engined classes as among the heavyweights, so technical restrictions are not the solution. Perhaps the active vetting and supervision of new riders, along the line of 'rooky tests' at Indianapolis, might avoid crashes due to inexperience, and this could be a valuable service that ex-riders could perform.

The Future of the TT

What was once the greatest international motorcycle race in the world is now a celebration of motorcycling in general. The races are part of a programme which includes Moto-cross, drag races, vintage rallies, one-make club meetings and a continuous display of spectators' own motorcycles, from the highly exotic to the unbelievably tatty.

The many side-attractions and the relaxed and friendly character of residents, including police, help make a visit to the TT memorable, but it is only the racing that is unique to the Isle of Man. No one suffers the Liverpool to Douglas crossing just to watch the Red Arrows or a Miss Wet T-shirt competition – or do they? I am convinced that the survival of the TT depends on continued racing over the Mountain Course – or at least over part of it. The organizers – the ACU and the Isle of Man Tourist Board – should concentrate their resources on the popularity and the stature of the road races, and with luck the names of Joey Dunlop and his successors will be legends in the 2000s, as much as Jimmy Guthrie, Geoff Duke and Mike Hailwood are now.

Australian Kel Carruthers won the 1969 Lightweight on a Benelli. He returned in 1970 to win on a Yamaha. He later controlled Yamaha racing activities in the USA, and developed Kenny Roberts as a rider. **(Mike Corrin)**

Agostini was a comfortable and experienced TT rider by 1970, when he won both the Junior and Senior races, making his total of wins seven. **(Mike Corrin)**

The 1970 Senior race. The Barnett-Williams battle in full swing on the way down to Creg-ny-Baa. Barnett has caught and passed Williams, (No. 3,) who is not letting him go. **(Mike Corrin)**

Peter Williams (Arter-Matchless) swings out of the Gooseneck after Barnett retired, to take second place in the Senior TT. Note the disc front brake and cast magnesium wheels pioneered by Williams. **(Mike Corrin)**

John Williams (Arter-Matchless) bounces at the bottom of Bray Hill on his way to fifth in the 1970 Senior. **(EMAP)**

Below: *Klaus Enders (BMW) leads Helmut Fath (URS) in Ramsey in the 1969 Sidecar TT. Enders won and Fath took third place.* **(Mike Corrin)**

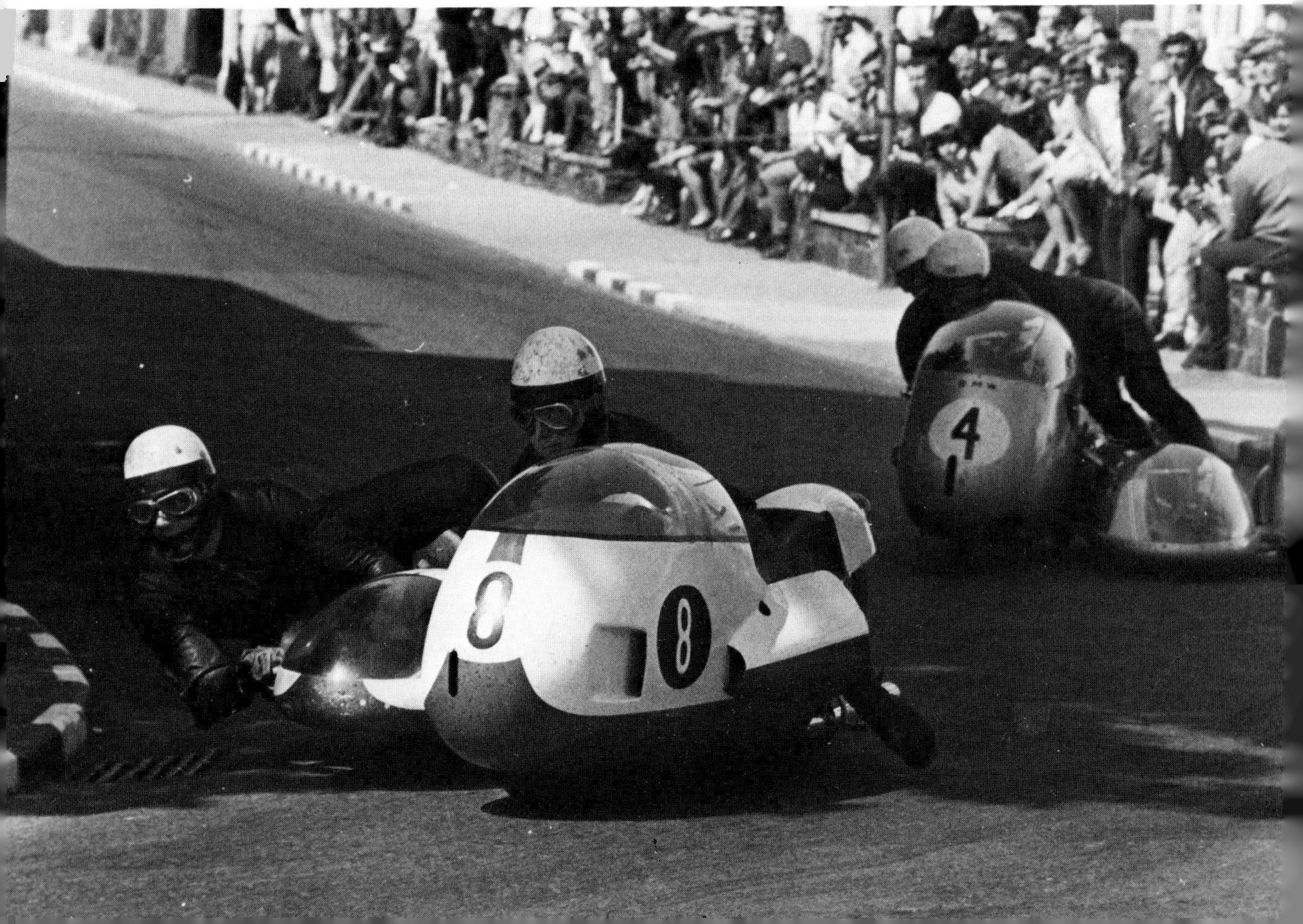

Siggi Schauzu in the air at Ballaugh in 1970, when he won the 750 class sidecar TT. In 11 TT races Schauzu only retired once, and he won 7. **(Dennis Reed)**

1973. Peter Williams on the John Player Norton in the year that he won the Formula 750 TT, turning in the fastest lap since Mike Hailwood's record lap in 1967. Williams averaged over 105 mph. **(EMAP)**

The Transatlantic match races of the 1970s saw American riders demonstrate 'wheelies', as they turned on 100 bhp at the back wheel. Californian Pat Hennen obliges Isle of Man photographer and pilot Dennis Reed with two during the 1977 Senior. Dennis gave Hennen, and other racers, an aerial preview of the Mountain Course. **(Dennis Reed)**

Hailwood's return in 1979 inspired the best in other riders. Here Ron Haslam takes White Gates in a full racing crouch on the big 998cc Honda in pursuit of Hailwood. **(Dennis Reed)**

The other Man of the 1979 Races was Alex George, who won the Formula One and Classic TT races. Here he is seen at Governor's Bridge with the 998cc works Honda.

Mike Hailwood in 1979: still fast, still graceful, he set a new lap record while winning the 500cc TT on this works-prepared Suzuki. (Mike Corrin)

Another stylish and incredibly fast rider, leaning off his Honda to transfer weight to his front wheel, Joey Dunlop banks well over during a recent TT. (Mike Corrin)

Trevor Ireson won both sidecar TT races at over 100 mph in 1979. Passenger Pollington looks relaxed as they take a tight line across Parliament Square. (Mike Corrin)

Jock Taylor and Benga Johansson won the fastest Sidecar TT leg from Ireson and Pollock in 1980. Here they take a wider line at the same point. (Mike Corrin)

Power and exuberance both under control in this fine shot by Mike Corrin of Joey Dunlop near Ballacraine.

Norton flies again! The reborn Norton company fielded this rotary-engined racer in the 1988 TT, ridden by Trevor Nation. While its performance was nothing special, it promised exciting things in the future. **(Mike Corrin)**

The magic of the Isle of Man TT, captured in this view of Steve Hislop catching the rotary Norton of Trevor Nation in 1989. Hislop lapped at over 120 mph before winning the race. **(Mike Corrin)**

Chapter 14:

A Gallery of Riders

Charlie and Harry Collier, two men who helped start and establish the Tourist Trophy races, then went on to win three of them between them. This picture is from 1911, when Harry finished second in the Junior TT on a Matchless, of course. He is on the right of the picture. **(EMAP)**

Although only 20, Victor Surridge was already a successful member of the Rudge team, having broken records at Brooklands, when he was entered for the 1911 TT. Surridge died in a practice crash, the first TT fatality; the Coroner advised shortening the course to make it easier for riders to remember each bend. **(Manx Museum)**

Jake de Rosier, already looking unhappy before the start of the first TT on the Mountain Course in 1911. De Rosier came from the United States, where he was a superb track racer, and made fastest lap in practice. His race was a series of mishaps and ended in his disqualification. **(Manx Museum)**

Oliver Godfrey won the first Mountain TT in 1911. The Indian he rode had chain drive and a strong gearbox at a time when variable pulleys and belt drive were more normal. **(Keig)**

Bert le Vack, designer, master-tuner, track racer and successful TT rider on one of the later Indians developed from the back cylinder of the V-twin in 1921 **(Keig)**

C. W. 'Paddy' Johnson raced on the Isle of Man from 1922 to 1951, winning the 1926 Lightweight and taking three second places, on Cottons. He is seen in 1923, showing off the characteristic straight-tube Cotton frame.

Right and opposite top: *Achille Varzi, already a fine racing driver in 1923 and to become one of the greatest ever with Alfa Romeo and Auto Union Grand Prix cars. Clearly a man of style both in 'civvies' and in racing attire, he is seen on the 1923 DOT-JAP and the 1924 DOT-Blackburne.*

George Dance retired in seven out of eight TTs that he started, often after breaking the lap record. Sprinting was his speciality and he stands behind the sprint Sunbeam, from which every spare ounce has been trimmed. **(VMCC)**

Freddie Dixon, for once looking a bit uncomfortable, at his wedding. Freddie was inventive, determined and tough and after an outstanding career as a racing motorcyclist, he was active as an engineer with such projects as the ERA racing car and the four-wheel-drive cars of Harry Ferguson. **(EMAP)**

Quiet, calculating and shrewd, Wal Handley had a reputation for a quick temper as well as a sense of humour. He contested 28 TT races, winning three, including the 1927 Lightweight (above). **(EMAP)**

Stanley Woods, the most successful TT rider until Mike Hailwood, looking happy after a well-judged race on a fine machine in the 1935 'Senior'.

The Sunbeam team prize winners in 1928. From the left: Arcangeli, Charlie Dodson and Franconi. Franconi only finished twice in nine TTs, while Arcangeli finished in four out of five, his best place being second in the 1927 Lightweight on a Moto Guzzi. (VMCC)

C. J. P. 'Charlie' Dodson on the 500cc Sunbeam that took him to fourth place in the 1930 Senior TT. Compare this machine with one of Varzi's DOTs to see how light weight gave way to sophistication.

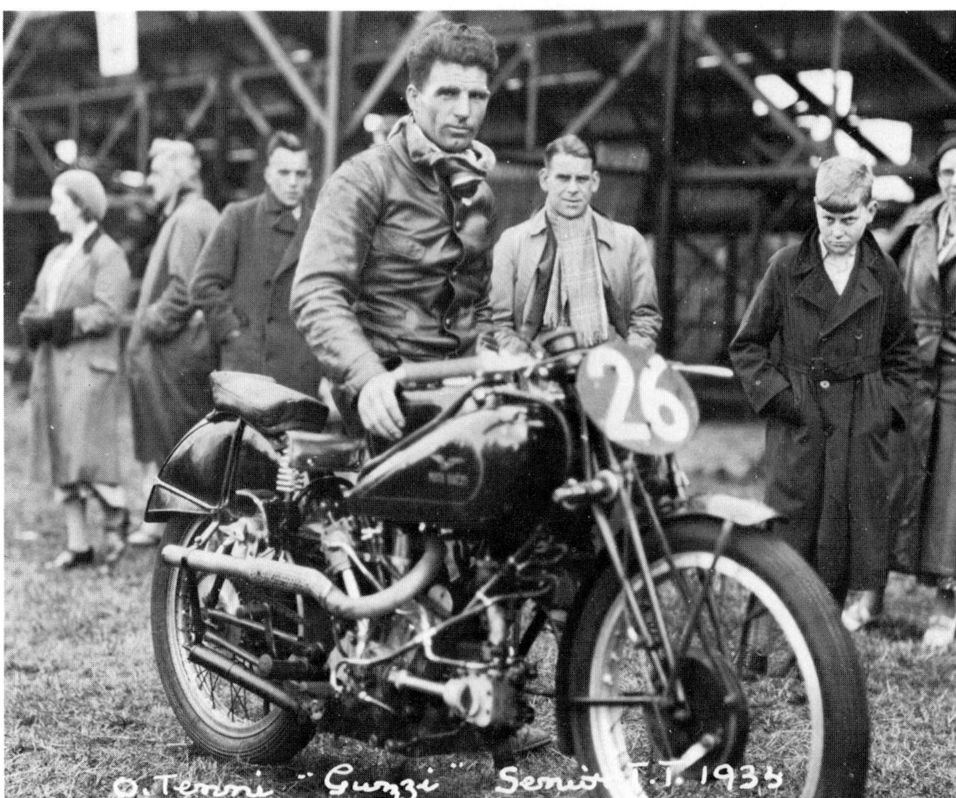

Omobono Tenni only raced in five TTs between 1935 and 1948, but he won his second (the 1937 Lightweight) and nearly won the 1948 Senior. Tenni was twice Champion of Italy, a popular hero and no respecter of convention. In 1935 he won the road race from Milan to Taranto on a Moto Guzzi V-twin, and in 1936 he was co-driver of the 2-litre class-winning Maserati in the Mille Miglia car race. **(Keig)**

J. H. White, known as 'Crasher' White after some early mishaps, was placed no lower than fifth in eight of his ten TTs. His contract with the German firm of NSU was limited to the 1939 Junior TT, this large unsprung machine being a 350, and he finished fifth in the Senior on a Norton. **(Keig)**

Dario Ambrosini was the only man to challenge the Guzzi team betwen 1949 and 1951. Here he warms up the 250 Benelli before the Lightweight TT in 1950, the year he won both the TT and the World Championship. **(Island Photographics)**

Fergus Anderson, a racer for 25 years and a great worker for better pay and safety for riders in the 1950s, uses two Guzzi team-mates as arm-rests in 1949. On the left is Bruno Ruffo, a superb rider and chief opponent of Ambrosini, and, on the right, Gianni Leoni. **(EMAP)**

Bob Foster rode many interesting machines between 1935 and 1951. He won the Lightweight in 1935 on a New Imperial and the Junior in 1947 on a Velocette. This is the works Guzzi on which he almost won the 1950 Senior TT. **(Keig)**

A great TT rider who only won one TT, Les Graham was World Champion in the 500cc class in 1949 and soldiered on with AJS until 1951. This is the 1951 shaft-drive MV Agusta that he helped develop into a competitive force. **(Keig)**

Geoff Duke smiles confidently as he takes the new 'Featherbed' Norton to the start of the 1950 Senior TT. He dominated racing for the next six years, racing Nortons and Gileras and winning the 500cc World Championship every year from 1950 to 1955. **(Keig)**

Lightweight Champions of the 1950s after the 1954 125cc TT: in the centre, Rupert Hollaus, on the left Werner Haas, 125 and 250 Champions respectively in 1954; on the right Carlo Ubbiali, second in the race. **(EMAP)**

Ray Amm, the quiet, fearless Rhodesian, with his wife and Joe Craig after winning the 1953 Senior TT. He also won the Junior that year. **(EMAP)**

Dickie Dale ignores his mechanic's helpful advice to scowl at Keig's photographer. This is 1957 and the motorcycle is the V-8 Moto Guzzi on which Dale finished fourth. Dale rode this amazing machine to its only win, at Imola in 1957. **(Keig)**

A happy shot of Mike Hailwood and Derek Minter at Brands Hatch in 1960. Minter won the 1962 Lightweight TT on a Honda, but his career was interrupted by several bad crashes. **(EMAP)**

The Classic TT 1980. Joey Dunlop, centre, won at 112.7 mph, Mick Grant (right) was second, and Ron Haslam (left) was third. Three great sportsmen, and all three complete masters of the most powerful TT machinery. **(EMAP)**

Chapter 15:

A Gallery of Machines

The state of the art in 1903. A. Werner before the start of the Paris-Madrid road race that was stopped at Rouen after several fatal accidents. (EMAP)

Signs of progress: the 1908 TT Matchless-JAP 6 hp with vertical overhead valves, battery and coil ignition, single-speed direct belt drive and pedals to help get up Creg Willey's. Everything, including N. Drury's shoes, is gleaming. **(VMCC)**

The 1909 Scott. Only the cylinder head was water-cooled on the first racing Scotts, but they already had telescopic front forks and the rear-mounted kick-start that was a sensation of the 1909 TT. Eric Myers, seen here, did not finish. **(EMAP)**

The 1913 Douglas ohv; a primitive gearbox and very light weight gave the pre-WWI TT Douglas a competitive edge, and H. Bashall won the 1912 Junior on one. This is E. Elwall. **(Keig)**

The 1913 Regal-Precision, one of the short-lived makes to appear in the large 1914 Senior TT entry list. The 492cc Precision engine was one of a range designed by F. E. Baker. **(Keig)**

The 1914 Scott was a very advanced machine with a water-cooled two-stroke engine with rotary valve induction. It had telescopic forks, sprung saddle actuating a fuel pressure pump, and the lowest centre of gravity of any machine in the race. **(EMAP)**

The classic side-valve Norton of 1921 with stirrup front brake and no frills. **(Keig)**

In 1922 the first of the overhead valve Nortons with a little drum brake and interesting handlebars made its debut. The large exhaust diameter indicates a free breathing engine. **(Keig)**

The first of the overhead camshaft Nortons of 1927–29. This Walter Moore design also introduced the cradle frame that gave Nortons their exceptional roadholding. Stanley Woods blasted the lap record in 1927, but Alec Bennett won on another Norton. **(Keig)**

Jimmy Guthrie in 1933, somewhere on Douglas Promenade on the ohc Norton designed by Arthur Carroll in 1930 and developed for a further 20 years to become the most successful racing motorcycle ever. **(Keig)**

***The last pre-war Norton with twin ohc engine, rear suspension (since 1936) and new telescopic forks seen in 1938. Freddie Frith looks pleased with it. Like Guthrie, he carries a plug spanner in the top of his boot.* (Keig)**

***The 1922 model was the least adventurous of Diamond's TT machines and used a 250cc JAP engine.* (Keig)**

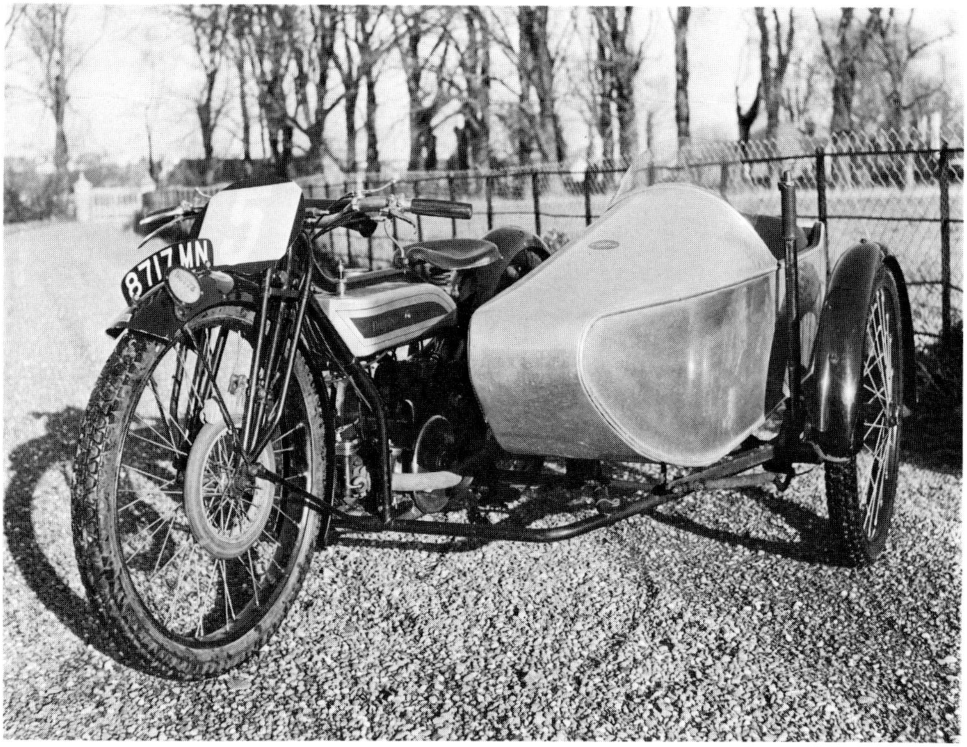

Freddie Dixon's winning Douglas sidecar outfit of 1923, complete with its unique banking chassis. The passenger pushed on the lever to lift the sidecar on right-hand bends, and pulled on it to lower the sidecar on left-handers. This fine outfit is now owned by a member of the VMCC and is usually on view at the National Motor Museum at Beaulieu.

The Beardmore Precision of 1924 – a courageous attempt to apply the latest automobile engine developments to a motorcycle engine; the Beardmore used a two-piece shaft to drive an overhead camshaft, with four valves, two carburettors and a magneto on top of the cylinder head. There were too many problems to sort out before the Junior TT, and push-rod engines were used in the race. **(VMCC)**

The 1926 New Hudson. It was a very modern machine for its year; the TT New Hudsons were prepared by Bert le Vack. Both drum brakes were foot-operated and a foot-lever also changed gear. Oliver Langton retired, but in 1927 Jimmy Guthrie finished second on a New Hudson. **(Keig)**

The 1936 DKW German complexity with a reed-valve version of the forced-induction DKW engine seen here with Stanley Woods. A forward-facing pumping piston drew from two carburettors (under the streamlined shells) to fill the double cylinder. The reed valves often broke, and in 1937 rotary valves were used instead. **(Keig)**

The 1937 Moto Guzzi. Italian simplicity, but the result of 14 years of racing development. Tenni's winning 250cc single had four valves per cylinder, swinging arm rear suspension, a large outside flywheel and the oil tank mounted on top of the fuel tank. **(Keig)**

The 1939 Benelli. The tiny firm of Benelli dated from 1911 and disputed Lightweight races with Moto Guzzi in the 1920s, 1930s and 1940s. The compact ohc single shown here with Ernie Mellors before his 1939 TT victory was their most successful design. It was also supercharged for some races. **(Keig)**

The 1939 AJS, a water-cooled V-four based on the 1935 sports AJS and fitted with supercharger and serpentine induction pipes. One of these racing dinosaurs has been rebuilt and can be seen at Sammy Miller's fine museum in Hampshire. Walter Rusk, here on the machine, achieved the first over 100 mph lap on a European road circuit at Ulster in 1939. **(Keig)**

The 1939 NSU. The fierce-looking supercharged parallel twins from Neckarsulm all failed to finish on the Isle of Man. There were several versions, this one with an unsprung rear wheel is straddled by Wilhelm Herz, who worked on the machines successfully after the war. Herz broke the motorcycle world speed record on a special version of the NSU in 1951. **(Keig)**

The 1939 Velocette. The supercharged parallel twin Velocette was finished too close to the 1939 TT to be raceworthy. This shot with Stanley Woods shows the bulbous crankcase which acted as an oil reservoir, and the shaft final drive. **(Keig)**

The Velocette Roarer on the test-bed. The ribbed supercharger and carburettor are at the rear end of the crankcase, the oil reservoir is nearest the camera, and the inlet pipes snaked over the cylinder head to the inlet ports at the front of the engine. A complete rebuild of this famous machine has been undertaken by Ivan Rhodes and his son, two Velocette devotees, in Derbyshire. **(VMCC)**

The 1939 BMW. BMW's Director of research, Rudolf Schleicher, produced a truly great racing machine in 1937, the supercharged 492cc twin. Its dry weight was only 305 lb, its top speed was over 140 mph, and on it Georg Meier won the 1938 European Championship as well as the 1939 Senior TT. Induction pipes led from the crankshaft-driven blower in front of the engine. Telescopic forks were standard on BMWs from 1935. **(Karl Reese)**

The 1950 V-twin Moto Guzzi, last of the type that first appeared in 1933. Notable are the massive drum brakes and dual brake levers under Bob Foster's right fingers, and the composite frame incorporating tubes, pressings and the crankcase. **(Keig)**

The first featherbed Manx Nortons, lined up before being shipped to the Isle of Man in 1950. These beautiful machines broke away from the stiff springing and angular lines of pre-war racers, and set new standards of road holding. **(EMAP)**

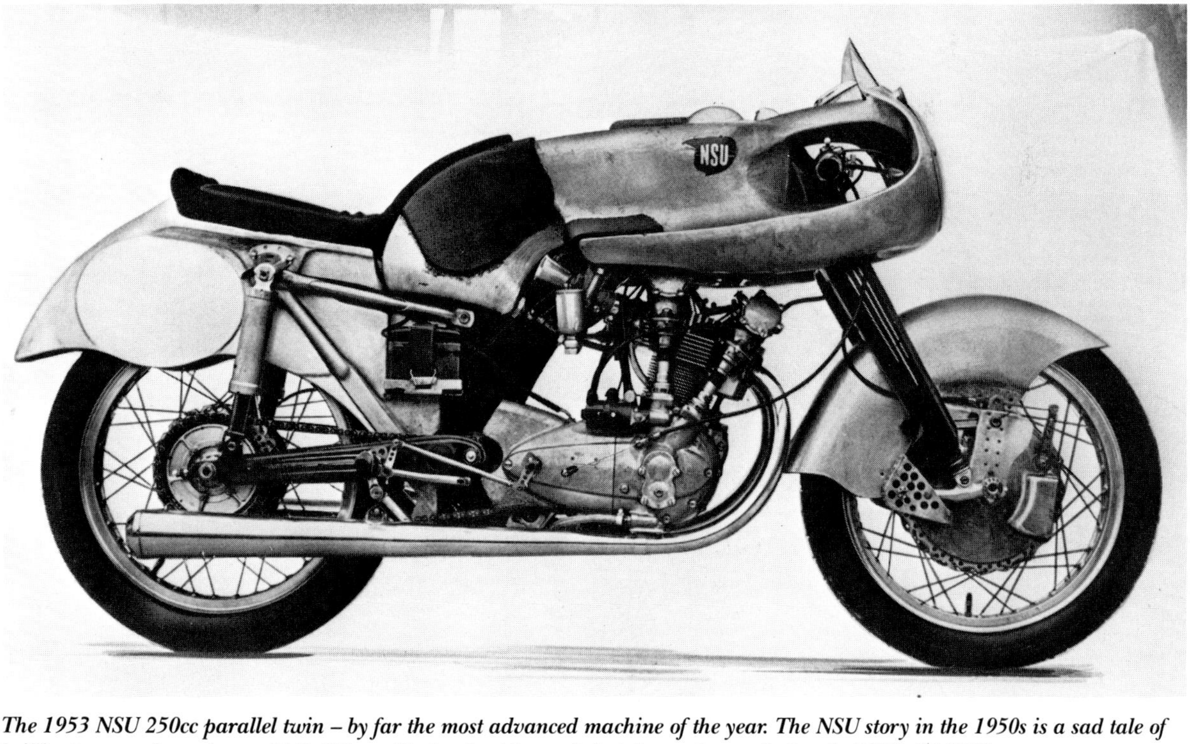

The 1953 NSU 250cc parallel twin – by far the most advanced machine of the year. The NSU story in the 1950s is a sad tale of brilliant success in racing, rapidly followed by bankruptcy and shut-down of manufacture in 1958. **(EMAP)**

The sidecar version of Norton's streamlined machine continued to achieve success long after the solo version had disappeared from sight. Here it is in 1954, clearly pointing the direction for racing sidecars right up to today. **(Keig)**

The development work of Les Graham was continued at MV Agusta by John Surtees and others, and for the best part of ten years from 1957 the 500cc MV was unbeatable. This is the 1960 version. **(EMAP)**

Japanese high-tech 1. The five-cylinder 125cc Honda engine whirled at a dizzy 19,000 rpm to develop 30 bhp at 125 mph. Exhaust pipes wind everywhere to make room for components. **(EMAP)**

Japanese high-tech 2. The 1968 Yamaha two-stroke V-4 with disc valves, resonance-tuned exhausts, water-cooling and about 58 bhp, making it among the fastest machines in any class. The 1968 version was less prone to seizure than earlier models. **(EMAP)**

100 bhp over the counter! The Yamaha TZ750 produced for sale to the braver independent rider in 1974 was crude compared to the 1968 works '250' and with four cylinders, reed valves and 750cc, it was not a dainty machine. **(EMAP)**

British low-tech. Who needs 100 bhp, tuned suspension and soft-compound tyres to race? G. S. Wakefield just turned down the handlebars of his Panther 250, took off its lights, and looks ready to take on the best before the 1950 Clubman's TT. **(Keig)**

Appendix: Results and Statistics of the TT

The Mountain Course – Progress of the Absolute Lap Record

1911	F. Philipp	(500 Scott)	44.52	50.148	Senior
1913	H.O. Wood	(500 Scott)	43.10	52.123	Senior
1914	H.O. Wood	(500 Scott)	42.16	53.233	Senior
1920	G. Dance	(500 Sunbeam)	40.43	55.628	Senior
1921	F.G. Edmond	(500 Triumph)	40.08	56.436	Senior
1922	A. Bennett	(500 Sunbeam)	37.46	59.973	Senior
1924	J.H. Simpson	(350 AJS)	35.05	64.541	Junior
1925	J.H. Simpson	(500 AJS)	32.50	68.964	Senior
1926	J.H. Simpson	(500 AJS)	32.09	70.429	Senior
1927	Stanley Woods	(500 Norton)	31.54	70.981	Senior
1929	C.J.P. Dodson	(500 Sunbeam)	30.47	73.556	Senior
1930	W.L. Handley	(Rudge)	29.41	76.282	Senior
1931	J.H. Simpson	(500 Norton)	28.01	80.820	Senior
1932	J.H. Simpson	(500 Norton)	27.47	81.499	Senior
1933	Stanley Woods	(500 Norton)	27.22	82.740	Senior
1935	Stanley Woods	(500 Guzzi)	26.10	86.534	Senior
1936	Stanley Woods	(500 Velocette)	26.02	86.977	Senior
1937	F.L. Frith	(500 Norton)	25.05	90.258	Senior
1938	H.L. Daniell	(500 Norton)	24.52.6	91.008	Senior
1950	G.E. Duke	(500 Norton)	24.16	93.33	Senior
1951	G.E. Duke	(500 Norton)	23.47	95.22	Senior
1953	W.R. Amm	(500 Norton)	23.15	97.41	Senior
1955	G.E. Duke	(500 Gilera)	22.39	99.97	Senior
1957	R.G. McIntyre	(500 Gilera)	22.23.4	101.12	Senior
1959	J. Surtees	(500 MV)	22.22.4	101.18	Senior
1060	J. Surtees	(500 MV)	21.45	104.08	Senior
1962	G.S. Hocking	(500 MV)	21.24.4	105.75	Senior
1963	S.M.B. Hailwood	(500 MV)	21.16.4	106.41	Senior
1966	S.M.B. Hailwood	(500 Honda)	21.08.6	107.07	Senior
1967	S.M.B. Hailwood	(500 Honda)	20.48.8	108.77	Senior
1975	M. Grant	(750 Kawasaki)	20.36.8	109.82	Classic
1976	J.G. Williams	(500 Suzuki)	20.09.8	112.27	Senior
1977	M. Grant	(750 Kawasaki)	20.04.4	112.77	Classic
1978	M. Grant	(750 Kawasaki)	19.48	114.33	Classic
1980	W.J. Dunlop	(750 Yamaha)	19.38.8	115.22	Classic

Senior TT Entries by Manufacturer,
1914, 1924, 1934, 1954, 1964 and 1979

1914

ABC(2)
Abingdon (3)
Alldays (3)
Ariel (3)
BSA (8)
Calthorpe (2)
Chase (1)
Douglas (3)
Dunkley (1)
Elswick Premier (1)
FN (2)
Indian (8)
Ivy Precision (4)
James (4)
Matchless (4)
Motosacoche (3)
Nestor (1)
New Hudson (1)
Norton (3)
NSU (3)
NUT (4)
Premier (4)
Puch (1)
Quadrant (3)
Regal Precision (2)
Rover (3)
Royal Ruby (2)
Rudge Multi (7)
Scott (4)
Singer (2)
Sunbeam (3)
Triumph (7)
Zenith (6)

TOTAL 108

1924

AJS (4)
Cotton (1)
Douglas (5)
Dot Bradshaw (1)
New Hudson (4)
Norton (10)
OEC-Blackbourn (1)
P&M (2)
Peugeot (3)
Scott (2)
Sunbeam (1)
Triumph (1)

TOTAL 35

1934

AJS (3)
Excelsior (3)
Eysinck (1)
Husqvarna (3)
New Imperial (2)
Norton (7)
OEC (2)
OK-Supreme-Jap (3)
Royal Enfield (1)
Rudge (2)
Sarolea (1)
Sunbeam (2)
Triumph (3)
Velocette (6)
Vincent-HRD-Jap (3)

TOTAL 42

1954

AJS (11)
BMW (1)
BSA (4)
FAN-Special (1)
Gilera (2)
Matchless (17)
MV Agusta (3)
Moto Guzzi (2)
Norton (44)
Velocette (3)

TOTAL 88

1964

ARC-BSA (1)
BSA (3)
BSA-Norton (1)
BMW (1)
Dunstall Dominator (1)
Fan-Special (1)
Gilera (2)
Matchless (29)
MV Agusta (1)
Norton (41)
Norton-Triumph (1)
RD Norvelo (1)
Springbok (1)
Triumph (5)

TOTAL 89

1979

Cagiva (1)
Honda (2)
Laverda (1)
Matchless (1)
Suzuki (29)
Yamaha (62)

TOTAL 96

Masters of the TT.
Winners of three or more International Tourist Trophy races
(Production Races not included).

R. Steinhausen	4	(1973–)
W.R. Amm	3	(1951–54)
H.L. Daniell	3	(1934–50)
T. Herron	3	(1973–77)
T. Ireson	3	(1969–)
W. Schneider	3	(1954–59)
L. Taveri	3	(1955–66)
R. McIntyre	3	(1953–62)
M. Deubel	3	(1960–66)
S.M. Hailwood	14	(1958–79)
G. Agostini	10	(1965–72)
S. Woods	10	(1922–39)
S. Schauzu	9	(1966–72)
P.W. Read	8	(1961–78)
C. Mortimer	7	(1968–)
C. Williams	7	(1971–)
A.J. Guthrie	6	(1923–37)
J. Surtees	6	(1954–60)
A.J. Redman	6	(1958–65)
A. Bennett	5	(1921–32)
G.E. Duke	5	(1950–59)
C. Ubialli	5	(1951–60)
F.L. Frith	4	(1936–49)
M. Grant	4	(1970–)
W. Handley	4	(1922–34)
T. Provini	4	(1955–65)

Tom Loughborough and the TT

From 1913 to 1939 responsibility for organizing the TT races lay almost entirely on the shoulders of one man, Tom Loughborough. As Secretary of the ACU, Tom not only redrafted TT regulations each year, wrote the annual report on the races to the ACU and sent out any Press releases, but also personally managed the races on the Isle of Man.

His hand-written notes in his copies of the TT Handbook range from the provision of ambulances to the choice of music for the PA, and from the settling of protests to the state of the Press tent. He was not a man to be trifled with (though it seems that Wal Handley tried his best) and Loughborough was quick to remove a marshal who was not up to the job or reprimand a rider who failed to stop when flagged off.

Here are some of Tom Loughborough's notes from the Isle of Man, capturing something of the atmosphere of the 1920s and 1930s.

Stewards' decision, 7.6.28.

'Handley to be reprimanded for declaring petrol & oil 47 hours late & cautioned not to repeat in Senior delay he had in getting his m/c out of depot in Lwt. Race'

Memoranda 1931

Scouts not to rush off until red lamp goes out.
Provision for tipped out oil & petrol in future years.
Small flaps for wreaths
Band still playing at 2nd signal
Slat above Dunlop ad
Gov's stand flowers
Medical tent filthy
Scoreboard to be raised 2'0" & fed from behind
Press tent dirty
Rubbish by Press Stairs
Mud in Press tent
Cardboard for Ebby's window

Stewards' Meeting.

10.6.33. Application from Handley no 15 Lwt Race for Mitchell to be allowed to start although not qualified. refused.

11.6.33. Harleyson repg. Handley & Parodi repg. Guzzi called & pleaded to EPG & self for reversal of above decision. Stewards considered question at 5.30... unanimously confirmed previous decision.

For several years Tom Loughborough kept a log of the progress of each race, pencilling in each decision and incident as the race unfolded, and some of these survive, carefully stuck in the back of his copy of the Handbook. I have reproduced his log of the 1929 Senior Race below, to the best of my ability, as his handwriting is sometimes unreadable.

This was the race when Handley pulled two badly hurt riders from the road at Greeba after a series of crashes, in which one of them, Lamb, was killed. Charlie Dodson (Sunbeam,) won. I have added the riders' names to Loughborough's cryptic notes. Otherwise they are just as he wrote them.

TT Races 1929

Log of Senior Race. 14th June

Time	No	Incident
9.47		Off. Car In
10.35	32	Off at Greeba requires doctor
		D. Lamb (Norton)
	15	is with 32 not hurt.
		W. Handley (AJS)
	32	all off at Greeba-v. slippery
10.42	42	15 restarted MO gone from Ballacraine
		J. Amott (Rudge)
	48	J. Simpson (Norton)
	8	no 8 record 31.30=71.881(x.998=71.74)
		Tyrell Smith (Rudge)
10.47	45	came off Creg Willys in Hotel think arm is broken
		H. Mathews (Norton)
		bruised forehead
10.50	45	Instructed Vict (?) explain Dr Fox how get Glen Helen hotel
10.52	41	Glen Helen Eng trouble OK
		J. Williams (Raleigh)
11.10	45	details of injuries-dis. shoulder. R. rib. slight head
11.40	30	retired at pits
		Porter (New Gerrard)
11.45	1	Eng. trouble Ballaugh OK
		F. Craner (Velo)
11.55	45	seen by doctor-slight concuss. superficial ambulance after race
12.1	8	Glen Helen. steering wrong (?)-ordered stop at pits ex
		Tyrell Smith (Rudge)
12.3	5	Ballig. slight injuries.
		T. Spann (AJS)
12.7	36	Pits eng. trouble
12.15	14	Sulby. OK
		T. Bullus (Raleigh)
12.20	45	Instructed B'craine to get 45 on stretcher or door by bearer party to Crosby
12.35	38	Bray Hill OK
		Chrystall (Grindlay)
12.35	12	Pits OK
		Simister (Velo)
12.33	45	Stenning advises re carrying 45 to Crosby
12.40	28	S. Woods. Kirk
		Woods (Norton)
12.55	6	Craig-ny-Baa OK
		D. Langton (Scott)
12.58	21	Kirk OK
		Twemlow (DOT)
1.11	1	Commenced his last lap
		C. Dodson (Sunbeam)
1.14	28	Dr reports chin cut & stitched up 1 or teeth out
		S. Woods (Norton)
1.16	35	at Bins
		Denney (Rudge)
1.17	47	at Balla Craine OK
		Mainwaring (Scott)
1.25	22	at Bins
		Potts (Grindlay)
1.34	46	at Ramsey OK
		G. Walker (Rudge)
1.42	23	at Bungalow OK
		Byrne (Norton)
1.48	1	now definitely wins at 72.05
		C. Dodson (Sunbeam)
1.50	18	just passed Craig touring
		Sarkis (OK Supreme)
1.56	3	Kirk Ignition OK
		Ghersi (Cotton)
2.10	1	reports OK by Prescott (?)
		Dodson
2.12	18	at Bins OK
		Sarkis
2.20		Sent ambulance along course to Greeba
2.20	7&19	at Bins
		S. G. Leave & G. Griffiths
2.34	40	?
		H. Pilling (Norton)
2.40		Sent off opening car from Ramsey
2.41	20	(touring past Kirk)
		P. Vare (Scott)
		Car in at 3.3 pm

Results and Statistics of the TT

Year	RACE Class	Miles	Rider	Machine	Time h.m.s.	Speed mph	Fastest Lap	Time m.s.	Speed mph
1907	**Twins**	158⅛	1 H. Rem Fowler	Norton	4.21.53	36.22	H. Rem Fowler (Norton)	22.06	42.91
			2 W. H. Wells	Vindec	4.53.04	32.21			
			3 W. M. Heaton	Rex	5.11.04	28.50			
	Singles	158⅛	1 C. R. Collier	Matchless	4.08.08	38.22	H. A Collier (Matchless)	23.05	41.81
			2 J. Marshall	Triumph	4.19.47	37.11			
			3 F. Hulbert	Triumph	4.27.50	35.89			
1908	**Twins**	158⅛	1 H. Reed	DOT	4.05.58	38.59	W. H. Bashall (BAT)	22.27	42.25
			2 W. H. Bashall	BAT	4.08.15	37.18			
			3 R. O. Clark	FN	4.11.03	36.19			
	Singles	158⅛	1 J. Marshall	Triumph	3.54.50	40.49	J. Marshall (Triumph)	22.20	42.48
			2 C. R. Collier	Matchless	3.57.07	40.01			
			3 Sir R. Arbuthnot	Triumph	4.07.57	38.22			
1909		158⅛	1 H. A. Collier	Matchless	3.13.37	49.01	H. A. Collier (Matchless)	18.05	52.27
			2 G. L. Evans	Indian	3.17.35	47.28			
			3 W. F. Newsome	Triumph	3.31.10	45.88			
1910		158⅛	1 C. R. Collier	Matchless	3.07.24	50.63	H. H. Bowen (BAT)	17.51	53.15
			2 H. A. Collier	Matchless	3.12.45	48.61			
			3 W. Creyton	Triumph	3.17.58	46.28			
1911	**Senior**	187½	1 O. C. Godfrey	Indian	3.56.10	47.63	F. Philipp (Scott)	44.52	50.11
			2 C. B. Franklin	Indian	3.59.52	46.81			
			3 A. Moorhouse	Indian	4.05.34	45.39			
	Junior	150	1 P. J. Evans	Humber	3.37.07	41.45	P. J. Evans (Humber)	53.24	42.00
			2 H. A. Collier	Matchless	3.46.20	40.09			
			3 H. J. Cox	Forward	3.55.56	38.23			
1912	**Senior**	187½	1 F. A. Applebee	Scott	3.51.08	48.69	F. A. Applebee (Scott)	45.31	49.44
			2 J. R. Haswell	Triumph	3.57.57	46.41			
			3 H. A. Collier	Matchless	4.01.56	44.89			
	Junior	150	1 W. H. Bashall	Douglas	3.46.59	39.65	E. Kickham (Douglas)	53.53	41.76
			2 E. Kickham	Douglas	3.51.36	37.58			
			3 H. J. Cox	Forward	4.06.29	34.27			
1913	**Senior**	262½	1 H. O. Wood	Scott	5.26.18	48.27	H. O. Wood (Scott)	43.10	52.12
			2 A. R. Abbott	Rudge	5.26.23	48.25			
			3 A. H. Alexander	Indian	5.30.11	46.10			
	Junior	225	1 H. Mason	NUT	5.08.34	43.75	H. Mason (NUT)	49.32	45.42
			2 W. F. Newsome	Douglas	5.09.30	43.69			
			3 H. C. Newman	Ivy Green	5.23.06	41.57			
1914	**Senior**	225	1 C. G. Pullin	Rudge	4.32.48	49.49	H. O. Wood (Scott)	42.16	53.50
			2 = H. R. Davies	Sunbeam	4.39.12	48.50			
			2 = O. C. Godfrey	Indian	4.39.12	48.50			
	Junior	187½	1 E. Williams	AJS	4.06.50	45.58	E. Williams (AJS)	47.18	47.57
			2 C. Williams	AJS	4.11.34	44.88			
			3 F. J. Walker	Royal Enfield	4.19.55	43.72			
1920	**Senior**	226½	1 T. C. De La Hay	Sunbeam	4.22.23	51.48	G. Dance (Sunbeam)	40.53	55.62
			2 D. M. Brown	Norton	4.26.15	51.00			
			3 W. R. Brown	Sunbeam	4.32.27	49.68			
	Junior 350 cc	187½	1 C. Williams	AJS	4.37.57	40.74	E. Williams (AJS)	44.06	51.36
			2 J. Watson-Bourne	Blackburne	4.47.07	39.10			
			3 J. Holroyd	Blackburne	4.47.37	39.09			
	Junior 250 cc	187½	1 R. O. Clark	Levis	4.55.37	38.30	R. O. Clark (Levis)	52.37	43.00
			2 G. Kuhn	Levis	–	35.61			
			3 F. W. Applebee	Levis	–	31.00			
1921	**Senior**	226½	1 H. R. Davies	350 cc AJS	4.09.22	54.50	F. G. Edmond (Triumph)	40.08	56.40
			2 F. W. Dixon	Indian	4.11.35	54.02			
			3 H. Le Vack	Indian	4.12.06	53.91			
	Junior 350 cc	187½	1 E. Williams	AJS	3.37.23	52.11	H. R. Davies (AJS)	41.04	55.15
			2 H. R. Davies	AJS	3.41.10	51.20			
			3 T. M. Sheard	AJS	3.49.09	49.42			
	Junior 250 cc	187½	1 D. G. Prentice	New Imperial	4.12.37	44.61	B. Kershaw (New Imperial)	49.07	46.11
			2 G. S. Davison	Levis	–	44.33			
			3 W. G. Harrison	Velocette	–	43.14			

Year	RACE Class	Miles	Rider	Machine	Time h.m.s.	Speed mph	Fastest Lap	Time m.s.	Speed mph
1922	**Senior**	226½	1 A. Bennett	Sunbeam	3.53.02	58.31	A. Bennett	37.46	59.99
			2 W. Brandish	Triumph	4.00.22	56.52	(Sunbeam)		
			3 H. Langman	Scott	4.02.14	56.09			
	Junior	187½	1 T. M. Sheard	AJS	3.26.38	54.75	H. Le Vack	40.07	56.46
			2 G. Grinton	AJS	3.37.17	53.00	(New Imperial)		
			3 J. Thomas	Sheffield Henderson	3.47.28	50.00			
	Light-	187½	1 G. S. Davison	Levis	3.46.56	49.89	W. L. Handley	44.24	51.00
	weight		2 D. Young	Rex-Acme	4.00.17	47.12	(OK)		
			3 S. J. Jones	Velocette	4.01.31	46.90			
1923	**Senior**	226½	1 T. M. Sheard	Douglas	4.04.43	55.55	J. Whalley	37.54	59.74
			2 G. M. Black	Norton	4.06.26	55.14	(Douglas)		
			3 F. W. Dixon	Indian	4.07.02	55.00			
	Junior	226½	1 S. Woods	Cotton	4.03.47	55.73	J. Simpson	38.00	59.59
			2 H. F. Harris	AJS	4.06.16	55.16	(AJS)		
			3 A. H. Alexander	Douglas	4.09.35	54.43			
	Light-	226½	1 J. A. Porter	New Gerrard	4.21.37	51.93	W. L. Handley	41.58	53.95
	weight		2 H. Le Vack	New Imperial	4.26.19	51.01	(OK)		
			3 D. Hall	Rex-Acme	4.34.20	49.53			
	Sidecar	113¼	1 F. W. Dixon	Douglas	2.07.48	53.15	H. Langman	41.24	54.69
			2 G. W. Walker	Norton	2.09.26	52.50	(Scott)		
			3 G. H. Tucker	Norton	2.10.27	52.07			
1924	**Senior**	226½	1 A. Bennett	Norton	3.40.24	61.64	F. W. Dixon	35.31	63.75
			2 H. Langman	Scott	3.41.51	61.23	(Douglas)		
			3 F. W. Dixon	Douglas	3.45.46	60.17			
	Junior	226½	1 K. Twemlow	New Imperial	4.04.21	55.67	J. H. Simpson	35.05	64.54
			2 S. Ollerhead	DOT	4.07.26	54.91	(AJS)		
			3 H. R. Scott	AJS	4.09.01	54.55			
	Light-	226½	1 E. Twemlow	New Imperial	4.05.03	55.44	E.Twemlow	38.51	58.28
	weight		2 H. F. Brockbank	Cotton	4.17.05	52.85	(New Imperial)		
			3 J. Cooke	DOT	4.18.33	52.54			
	Ultra	113¼	1 J. A. Porter	New Gerrard	2.12.40	51.20	J. A. Porter	43.02	52.61
	Light-		2 F. G. Morgan	Cotton	2.17.11	49.51	(New Gerrard)		
	weight		3 C. Stead	Cotton	2.17.39	49.34			
	Sidecar	151	1 G. H. Tucker	Norton	2.56.31	51.31	F. W. Dixon	42.32	53.23
			2 H. Reed	DOT	3.26.46	43.80	(Douglas)		
			3 A. Tinkler	Matador	3.33.03	42.49			
1925	**Senior**	226½	1 H. R. Davies	HRD	3.25.25.8	66.13	J.H. Simpson	32.50	68.97
			2 F. A. Longman	AJS	3.29.10	64.95	(AJS)		
			3 A. Bennett	Norton	3.30.08	64.65			
	Junior	226½	1 W. L. Handley	Rex-Acme	3.28.56.4	65.02	W. L. Handley	34.23	65.89
			2 H. R. Davies	HRD	3.32.42.2	63.87	(Rex-Acme)		
			3 J. H. Simpson	AJS	3.33.22.2	63.67			
	Light-	226½	1 E. Twemlow	New Imperial	3.55.18	57.74	W. L. Handley	37.36	60.22
	weight		2 C. W. Johnston	Cotton	3.58.51	56.88	(Rex-Acme)		
			3 K. Twemlow	New Imperial	4.03.19	55.83			
	Ultra	151	1 W. L. Handley	Rex-Acme	2.49.27	53.45	W. L. Handley	41.52	54.12
	Light-		2 C. W. Johnston	Cotton	2.53.54	52.08	(Rex-Acme)		
	weight		3 J. A. Porter	New Gerrard	2.57.40	50.98			
	Sidecar	151	1 L. Parker	Douglas	2.44.01.8	55.22	F. W. Dixon	39.36	57.18
			2 A. E. Taylor	Norton	2.45.58	54.57	(Douglas)		
			3 G. Grinton	Norton	2.46.45	54.31			
1926	**Senior**	264½	1 S. Woods	Norton	3.54.39.8	67.54	J. H. Simpson	32.09	70.43
			2 W. L. Handley	Rex-Acme	3.59.00.4	66.31	(AJS)		
			3 F. A. Longman	AJS	4.00.03.4	66.03			
	Junior	264¼	1 A. Bennett	Velocette	3.57.37	66.70	A. Bennett	32.56	68.75
			2 J. H. Simpson	AJS	4.08.02	63.90	(Velocette)		
			3 W. L. Handley	Rex-Acme	4.10.06	63.37			
	Light-	264¼	1. C. W. Jonhnston	Cotton	4.23.16.4	60.20	P. Ghersi	35.49	63.12
	weight		2 F. G. Morgan	Cotton	4.47.30.4	55.15	(Guzzi)		
			3 W. Colgan	Cotton	4.56.05	53.53			

Year	RACE Class	Miles	Rider	Machine	Time h.m.s.	Speed mph	Fastest Lap	Time m.s.	Speed mph
1927	**Senior**	264¼	1 A. Bennett	Norton	3.51.42	68.41	S. Woods	31.54	70.90
			2 J. Guthrie	New Hudson	4.00.04	66.02	(Norton)		
			3 T. Simister	Triumph	4.01.03	65.75			
	Junior	264¼	1 F. W. Dixon	HRD	3.55.54	67.19	W. L. Handley	32.44	69.18
			2 H. J. Willis	Velocette	4.04.39	64.78	(Rex-Acme)		
			3 J. H. Simpson	AJS	4.04.52	64.33			
	Light-weight	264¼	1 W. L. Handley	Rex-Acme	4.10.22	63.30	A. Bennett	35.08	64.45
			2 L. Archangeli	Guzzi	4.18.52	61.22	(OK-Supreme)		
			3 C. T. Ashby	OK-Supreme	4.19.24	61.10			
1928	**Senior**	264¼	1 C. J. P. Dodson	Sunbeam	4.11.40	62.98	J. H. Simpson	32.20	67.94
			2 G. E. Rowley	AJS	4.18.41	61.27	(AJS)		
			3 T. L. Hatch	Scott	4.20.18	60.89			
	Junior	264¼	1 A. Bennett	Velocette	3.50.52	68.65	A. Bennett	32.13	70.28
			2 H. J. Willis	Velocette	3.56.00	67.16	(Velocette)		
			3 K. Twemlow	DOT	4.08.57	63.67			
	Light-weight	264¼	1 F. A. Longman	OK-Supreme	4.11.59	62.90	F. A. Longman	35.08	64.45
			2 C. S. Barrow	Royal Enfield	4.29.01	58.92	(OK-Supreme)		
			3 E. Twemlow	DOT	4.29.26	58.83			
1929	**Senior**	264¼	1 C. J. P. Dodson	Sunbeam	3.39.59	72.05	C. J. P. Dodson	30.47	73.55
			2 A. Bennett	Sunbeam	3.44.47	70.51	(Sunbeam)		
			3 H. G. Tyrell-Smith	Rudge	3.45.37	70.25			
	Junior	264¼	1 F. G. HIcks	Velocette	3.47.23	69.71	F. G. Hicks	31.55	70.95
			2 W. L. Handley	AJS	3.48.45	69.29	(Velocette)		
			3 A. Bennett	Velocette	3.49.42	68.97			
	Light-weight	264¼	1 S. A. Crabtree	Excelsior	4.08.10	63.87	P. Ghersi	35.49	63.12
			2 K. Twemlow	DOT	4.13.25	62.55	(Guzzi)		
			3 F. A. Longman	OK-Supreme	4.16.33	61.78			
1930	**Senior**	264¼	1 W. L. Handley	Rudge	3.33.30	74.24	W. L. Handley	29.41	76.28
			2 G. W. Walker	Rudge	3.36.49	73.10	(Rudge)		
			3 J. H. Simpson	Norton	3.38.01	72.70			
	Junior	246¼	1 H. G. Tyrell-Smith	Rudge	3.43.00	71.08	G. E. Nott	31.21	72.2
			2 G. E. Nott	Rudge	3.43.35	70.89	(Rudge)		
			3 G. W. Walker	Rudge	3.43.58	70.77			
	Light-weight	264¼	1 A. J. Guthrie	AJS	4.04.56	64.71	W. L. Handley	33.52	66.86
			2 C. W. Johnston	OK-Supreme	4.07.23	64.07	(Rex-Acme)		
			3 C. S. Barrow	OK-Supreme	4.09.27	63.54			
1931	**Senior**	264¼	1 P. Hunt	Norton	3.23.28	77.90	J. H. Simpson	28.01	80.82
			2 A. J. Guthrie	Norton	3.24.57	77.34	(Norton)		
			3 S. Woods	Norton	3.27.36	76.35			
	Junior	264¼	1 P. Hunt	Norton	3.34.21	73.94	P. Hunt	30.05	75.27
			2 A. J. Guthrie	Norton	3.37.26	72.90	(Norton)		
			3 G. E. Nott	Rudge	3.39.01	72.37			
	Light-weight	264¼	1 G. W. Walker	Rudge	3.49.47	68.98	G. E. Nott	31.34	71.73
			2 H. G. Tyrell-Smith	Rudge	3.52.13	68.26	(Rudge)		
			3 E. A Mellors	New Imperial	3.57.08	66.84			
1932	**Senior**	264¼	1 S. Woods	Norton	3.19.40	79.38	J. H. Simpson	27.47	81.50
			2 A. J. Guthrie	Norton	3.21.59	78.47	(Norton)		
			3 J. H. Simpson	Norton	3.22.13	78.38			
	Junior	264¼	1 S. Woods	Norton	3.25.25	77.16	S. Woods	28.48	78.62
			2 W. L. Handley	Rudge	3.27.35	76.36	(Norton)		
			3 H. G. Tyrell-Smith	Rudge	3.34.08	74.02			
	Light-weight	264¼	1 L. H. Davenport	New Imperial	3.44.53	70.48	W. L. Handley	30.34	74.08
			2 G. W. Walker	Rudge	3.46.13	70.07	(Rudge)		
			3 W. L. Handley	Rudge	3.46.53	69.86			
1933	**Senior**	264¼	1 S. Woods	Norton	3.15.35	81.04	S. Woods	27.22	82.74
			2 J. H. Simpson	Norton	3.17.07	80.41	(Norton)		
			3 P Hunt	Norton	3.17.43	80.16			
	Junior	264¼	1 S. Woods	Norton	3.23.00	78.08	S. Woods	28.35	79.22
			2 P. Hunt	Norton	3.23.07	78.03	(Norton)		
			3 A. J. Guthrie	Norton	3.26.56	76.59			

Year	RACE Class	Miles	Rider	Machine	Time h.m.s.	Speed mph	Fastest Lap	Time m.s.	Speed mph
1933	**Lightweight**	264¼	1 S. Gleave	Excelsior	3.41.23	71.59	S. Gleave	31.11	72.62
			2 C. J. P. Dodson	New Imperial	3.43.43	70.85	(Excelsior)		
			3 C. H. Manders	Rudge	3.49.08	69.17			
1934	**Senior**	264¼	1 A. J. Guthrie	Norton	3.23.10	78.01	S. Woods	28.08	80.49
			2 J. H. Simpson	Norton	3.30.35	75.27	(Husqvarna)		
			3 W. F. Rusk	Velocette	3.36.19	73.27			
	Junior	264¼	1 A. J. Guthrie	Norton	3.20.14	79.16	A. J. Guthrie	28.16	80.11
			2 J. H. Simpson	Norton	3.20.23	79.10	(Rudge)		
			3 G. E. Nott	Husqvarna	3.26.02	76.93			
	Lightweight	264¼	1 J. H. Simpson	Rudge	3.43.50	70.81	J. H. Simpson	30.45	73.64
			2 G. E. Nott	Rudge	3.47.07	69.76	(Rudge)		
			3 G. W. Walker	Rudge	3.54.13	67.67			
1935	**Senior**	264¼	1 S. Woods	Guzzi	3.07.10	84.68	S. Woods	26.10	86.53
			2 A. J. Guthrie	Norton	3.07.11	84.65	(Guzzi)		
			3 W. F. Rusk	Norton	3.09.45	83.53			
	Junior	264¼	1 A. J. Guthrie	Norton	3.20.16	79.14	W. F. Rusk	28.19	79.96
			2 W. F. Rusk	Norton	3.21.22	78.71	(Norton)		
			3 J. H. White	Norton	3.22.42	78.19			
	Lightweight	264¼	1 S. Woods	Guzzi	3.41.29	71.56	S. Woods	30.31	74.19
			2 H. G. Tyrell-Smith	Rudge	3.44.17	70.67	(Guzzi)		
			3 G. E. Nott	Rudge	3.48.30	69.37			
1936	**Senior**	264¼	1 A. J. Guthrie	Norton	3.04.43	85.80	S. Woods	26.02	86.98
			2 S. Woods	Velocette	3.05.01	85.66	(Velocette)		
			3 F. L. Frith	Norton	3.07.35	84.49			
	Junior	264¼	1 F. L. Frith	Norton	3.17.46	80.14	F. L. Frith	27.38	81.94
			2 J. H. White	Norton	3.23.16	77.97	(Norton)		
			3 E. A. Mellors	Velocette	3.23.25	77.91			
	Lightweight	264¼	1 A. R. Foster	New Imperial	3.33.22	74.28	S. Woods	29.43	76.20
			2 H. G. Tyrell-Smith	Excelsior	3.38.34	72.51	(SKW)		
			3 A. Geiss	DKW	3.38.37	72.49			
1937	**Senior**	264¼	1 F. L. Frith	Norton	2.59.41	88.21	F. L. Frith	25.05	90.27
			2 S. Woods	Velocette	2.59.56	88.09	(Norton)		
			3 J. H. White	Norton	3.08.44	83.97			
	Junior	264¼	1 A. J. Guthrie	Norton	3.07.42	84.43	F. L. Frith &	26.35	85.18
			2 F. L. Frith	Norton	3.10.17	83.29	A. J. Guthrie		
			3 J. H. White	Norton	3.12.00	82.54	(Norton)		
	Lightweight	264¼	1 O. Tenni	Guzzi	3.32.06	74.72	O. Tenni	29.08	77.72
			2 S. Wood	Excelsior	3.32.43	74.50	(Guzzi)		
			3 E. R. Thomas	DKW	3.36.36	73.17			
1938	**Senior**	264¼	1 H. L. Daniell	Norton	2.57.50.6	89.11	H. L. Daniell	24.52.6	91.00
			2 S. Woods	Velocette	2.58.05.8	88.99	(Norton)		
			3 F. L. Frith	Norton	2.58.07.4	88.98			
	Junior	264¼	1 S. Woods	Velocette	3.08.30	84.08	S. Woods	26.33	85.30
			2 E. A. Mellors	Velocette	3.12.20	82.40	(Velocette)		
			3 F. L. Frith	Norton	3.12.27	82.35			
	Lightweight	264¼	1 E. Kluge	DKW	3.21.56	78.48	E. Kluge	28.11	80.35
			2 S. Wood	Excelsior	3.33.05	74.38	(DKW)		
			3 H. G. Tyrell-Smith	Excelsior	3.35.16	73.62			
1939	**Senior**	264¼	1 G. Meier	BMW	2.57.19	89.38	G. Meier	24.57	90.75
			2 J. M. West	BMW	2.59.39	88.22	(BMW)		
			3 F. L. Frith	Norton	3.00.11	87.96			
	Junior	264¼	1 S. Woods	Velocette	3.10.10	83.19	H. L. Daniell	26.38	85.05
			2 H. L. Daniell	Norton	3.10.38	83.13	(Norton)		
			3 H. Fleischmann	DKW	3.12.05	82.51			
	Lightweight	264¼	1 E. A. Mellors	Benelli	3.33.26	74.25	S. Woods	28.58	78.16
			2 E. Kluge	DKW	3.37.11	72.97	(Guzzi)		
			3 H. G. Tyrell-Smith	Excelsior	3.40.3	71.91			
1947	**Senior**	264¼	1 H. L. Daniell	Norton	3.11.22.2	82.81	A. J. Bell (Norton)	26.56	84.07
			2 A. J. Bell	Norton	3.11.44.2	82.66	P. J. Goodman		
			3 P. J. Goodman	Velocette	3.12.11	82.46	(Velocette)		

Year	RACE Class	Miles	Rider	Machine	Time h.m.s.	Speed mph	Fastest Lap	Time m.s.	Speed mph
1947	**Junior**	264¼	1 A. R. Foster	Velocette	3.17.20	80.31	M. D. Whitworth	27.45	81.61
			2 M. D. Whitworth	Velocette	3.21.26	78.68	(Velocette)		
			3 J. A. Weddell	Velocette	3.28.07	76.15			
	Light-weight	264¼	1 M. Barrington	Guzzi	3.36.26.6	73.22	M. Cann	30.17	74.78
			2 M. Cann	Guzzi	3.37.10.8	72.97	(Guzzi)		
			3 B. Drinkwater	Excelsior	3.45.57	70.14			
1948	**Senior**	264¼	1 A. J. Bell	Norton	3.06.31	84.97	O. Tenni	25.43	88.06
			2 W. Doran	Norton	3.17.16	80.34	(Guzzi)		
			3 J. A. Weddell	Norton	3.19.11.2	79.56			
	Junior	264¼	1 F. L. Frith	Velocette	3.14.33.6	81.45	F. L. Firth	27.28	82.45
			2 A. R. Foster	Velocette	3.19.12.6	79.55	(Velocette)		
			3 A. J. Bell	Norton	3.20.50.6	78.91			
	Light-weight	264¼	1 M. Cann	Guzzi	3.30.49	75.18	M. Cann	29.31	76.72
			2 R. H. Pike	Rudge	3.40.33.4	71.86	(Guzzi)		
			3 D. St. J. Beasley	Excelsior	3.54.09	67.68			
1949	**Senior**	264¼	1 H. Daniell	Norton	3. 2.18.6	86.93	A. R. Foster	25.14	89.75
			2 R. St. J. Lockett	Norton	3. 3.52.4	86.19	(Guzzi)		
			3 E. Lyons	Velocette	3. 5.22	85.50			
	Junior	264¼	1 F. L. Frith	Velocette	3.10.36	83.15	F. L. Frith	26.53	84.23
			2 E. Lyons	Velocette	3.11.08	82.92	(Velocette)		
			3 A. J. Bell	Norton	3.11.49	82.62			
	Light-weight	264¼	1 M. Barrington	Guzzi	3.23.13.2	77.96	R. H. Dale &	28.09	80.44
			2 T. L. Wood	Guzzi	3.23.25.8	77.91	T. L. Wood		
			3 R. H. Pike	Rudge	3.37.42.6	72.79	(Guzzi)		
1950	**Senior**	264¼	1 G. E. Duke	Norton	2.51.45.6	92.27	G. E. Duke	24.16	93.33
			2 A. J. Bell	Norton	2.54.25.6	90.85	(Norton)		
			3 R. St. J. Lockett	Norton	2.55.22.4	90.37			
	Junior	264¼	1 A. J. Bell	Norton	3.03.35	86.33	A. J. Bell	25.56	86.49
			2 G. E. Duke	Norton	3.04.52	85.73	(Norton)		
			3 H. L. Daniell	Norton	3.07.56	84.33			
	Light-weight	264¼	1 D. Ambrosini	Benelli	3.22.58	78.08	D. Ambrosini	27.59	80.91
			2 M. Cann	Guzzi	3.22.58.2	78.07	(Benelli)		
			3 R. A. Mead	Velocette	3.29.38	75.60			
1951	**Senior**	264¼	1 G. E. Duke	Norton	2.48.56.8	93.83	G. E. Duke	23.47	95.22
			2 W. Doran	AJS	2.53.19.2	91.44	(Norton)		
			3 W. McCandless	Norton	2.55.27	90.33			
	Junior	264¼	1 G. E. Duke	Norton	2.56.17.6	89.90	G. E. Duke	24.47	91.38
			2 R. St. J. Lockett	Norton	2.59.35	88.25	(Norton)		
			3 J. Brett	Norton	3.00.22.4	87.87			
	Light-weight 250 cc	151	1 T. L. Wood	Guzzi	1.51.15.8	81.39	F. K. Anderson	27.03	83.70
			2 D. Ambrosini	Benelli	1.51.24.2	81.29	(Guzzi)		
			3 E. Lorenzetti	Guzzi	1.55.00	78.75			
	Light-weight 125 cc	75½	1 W. McCandless	Mondial	1.00.30	74.85	W. McCandless	30.03	75.34
			2 C. Ubbiali	Mondial	1.00.52.4	74.38	(Mondial)		
			3 G. Leoni	Mondial	1.03.19.8	71.52			
1952	**Senior**	264¼	1 H. R. Armstrong	Norton	2.50.28.4	92.97	G. E. Duke	23.52	94.88
			2 R. L. Graham	MV	2.50.55	92.72	(Norton)		
			3 W. R. Amm	Norton	2.51.31.2	92.40			
	Junior	264¼	1 G. E. Duke	Norton	2.55.30.6	90.29	G. E. Duke	24.53	91.00
			2 H. E. Armstrong	Norton	2.56.57.8	89.55	(Norton)		
			3 R. W. Coleman	AJS	2.58.12.4	88.93			
	Light-weight 250 cc	151	1 F. K. Anderson	Guzzi	1.48.08.6	83.82	B. Ruffo	26.42	84.82
			2 E. Lorenzetti	Guzzi	1.48.40.8	83.36	(Guzzi)		
			3 S. Lawson	Guzzi	1.49.43.2	82.54			
	Light-weight 125 cc	113¼	1 C. C. Sandford	MV	1.29.54.8	75.54	C. C. Sandford	29.46	76.07
			2 C. Ubbiali	Mondial	1.31.35	74.16	(MV)		
			3 A. L. Parry	Mondial	1.34.02.6	72.22			
1953	**Senior**	264¼	1 W. R. Amm	Norton	2.48.51.8	93.85	W. R. Amm	23.15	97.41
			2 J. Brett	Norton	2.49.03.8	93.74	(Norton)		
			3 H. R. Armstrong	Gilera	2.49.16.8	93.62			

Year	RACE Class	Miles	Rider	Machine	Time h.m.s.	Speed mph	Fastest Lap	Time m.s.	Speed mph
1953	**Junior**	264¼	1 W. R. Amm	Norton	2.55.05	90.52	W. R. Amm	24.40	91.82
			2 K. T. Kavanagh	Norton	2.55.14.6	90.44	(Norton)		
			3 F. K. Anderson	Guzzi	2.57.40.6	89.41			
	Light-weight 250 cc	151	1 F. K. Anderson	Guzzi	1.46.53	84.73	F. K. Anderson	26.29	85.52
			2 W. Haas	NSU	1.47.10	84.52	(Guzzi)		
			3 S. Wunsche	DKW	1.51.20	81.34			
	Light-weight 125 cc	113¼	1 R. L. Graham	MV	1.27.19	77.79	R. L. Graham	28.57	78.21
			2 W. Haas	NSU	1.28.00	77.18	(MV)		
			3 C. C. Sandford	MV	1.28.02	77.15			
1954	**Senior**	151	1 W. R. Amm	Norton	1.42.46.8	88.12	W. R. Amm	25.12.8	89.82
			2 G. E. Duke	Gilera	1.43.52.6	87.19	(Norton)		
			3 J. Brett	Norton	1.45.15.2	86.04			
	Junior	188¾	1 R. Coleman	AJS	2. 3.41.8	91.51	W. R. Amm	23.56	94.61
			2 D. Farrant	AJS	2. 5.31	90.15	(Norton)		
			3 R. D. keeler	Norton	2. 5.43.6	90.03			
	Light-weight 250 cc	113¼	1 W. Haas	NSU	1.14.44.4	90.88	W. Haas	24.49.4	91.22
			2 R. Hollaus	NSU	1.15.28.6	89.99	(NSU)		
			3 H. R. Armstrong	NSU	1.15.31.8	89.92			
	Light-weight 125 cc	114	1 R. Hollaus	NSU	1.33.03.4	69.57	R. Hollaus	9.03.4	71.53
			2 C. Ubbiali	MV	1.33.07.4	69.52	(NSU)		
			3 C. C. Sandford	MV	1.37.35.8	66.35			
	Sidecar	114	1 E. Oliver	Norton	1.34.00.2	68.87	E. Oliver	9.09	70.85
			2 F. Hillebrand	BMW	1.35.56.2	67.48	(Norton)		
			3 W. Noll	BMW	1.39.16.4	65.22			
1955	**Senior**	264¼	1 G. E. Duke	Gilera	2.41.49.8	97.93	G. E. Duke	22.39	99.97
			2 H. R. Armstrong	Gilera	2.43.49	96.74	(Gilera)		
			3 K. T. Kavanagh	Guzzi	2.46.32.8	95.16			
	Junior	264¼	1 W. A. Lomas	Guzzi	2.51.38.2	92.33	W. A. Lomas	24.03.2	94.13
			2 R. McIntyre	Norton	2.52.38.2	91.79	(Guzzi)		
			3 C. C. Sandford	Guzzi	2.53.02.2	91.59			
	Light-weight 250 cc	97	1 W. A. Lomas	MV	1.21.38.2	71.37	W. A. Lomas	8.52	73.13
			2 C. C. Sandford	Guzzi	1.22.29.4	70.63	(MV)		
			3 H. P. Muller	NSU	1.26.21.6	67.47			
	Light-weight 125 cc	97	1 C. Ubbiali	MV	1.23.38.2	69.67	C. Ubbiali	9.02.2	71.65
			2 L. Taveri	MV	1.23.40.2	69.64	(MV)		
			3 G. Lattanzi	Mondial	1.25.53	67.84			
	Sidecar	97	1 W. Schneider	BMW	1.23.14	70.01	W. Noll	9.00	71.93
			2 W. G. Boddice	Norton	1.26.58.6	66.69	(BMW)		
			3 P. V. Harris	Matchless	1.28.22	65.94			
1956	**Senior**	264¼	1 J. Surtees	MV	2.44.05.8	96.57	J. Surtees	23.09.4	97.79
			2 J. Hartle	Norton	2.45.36.6	95.69	(MV)		
			3 J. Brett	Norton	2.46.54.2	94.96			
	Junior	264¼	1 K. T. Kavanagh	Guzzi	2.57.29.4	89.29	K. T. Kavanagh	24.18.8	93.15
			2 D. Ennett	AJS	3.02.07.4	87.02	(Guzzi)		
			3 J. Hartle	Norton	3.04.48.6·	85.75			
	Light-weight 250 cc	97	1 C. Ubbiali	MV	1.26.54.0	67.05	H. Baltisberger	9.21.6	69.17
			2 R. Colombo	MV	1.29.02.6	65.43	(NSU)		
			3 H. Baltisberger	NSU	1.29.24.6	65.17			
	Light-weight 125 cc	97	1 C. Ubbiali	MV	1.24.16.8	69.13	C. Ubbiali	9.09.8	70.65
			2 M. Cama	Montesa	1.29.19.2	65.24	(MV)		
			3 F. Gonzalez	Montesa	1.35.18.8	61.13			
	Sidecar	97	1 F. Hillebrand	BMW	1.23.12.2	70.03	W. Noll	9.01.6	71.12
			2 P. V. Harris	Norton	1.24.47.8	68.71	(BMW)		
			3 W. Boddice	Norton	1.26.19.2	67.50			
1957	**Senior**	302	1 R. McIntyre	Gilera	3.02.57.0	98.99	R. McIntyre	22.23.2	101.12
			2 J. Surtees	MV	3.05.04.2	97.86	(Gilera)		
			3 R. N. Brown	Gilera	3.09.02.0	95.81			
	Junior	264¼	1 R. McIntyre	Gilera	2.46.50.2	94.99	R. McIntyre	23.14.2	97.42
			2 K. Campbell	Guzzi	2.50.29.8	92.95	(Gilera)		
			3 R. N. Brown	Gilera	2.51.38.2	92.34			

Year	RACE Class	Miles	Rider	Machine	Time h.m.s.	Speed mph	Fastest Lap	Time m.s.	Speed mph
1957	**Light-weight 250 cc**	107½	1 C. C. Sandford	Mondial	1.25.25.4	75.80	T. Provini (Mondial)	8.18.0	78.00
			2 L. Taveri	MV	1.27.12.4	74.24			
			3 R. Colombo	MV	1.27.21.8	74.10			
	Light-weight 125 cc	107½	1 T. Provini	Mondial	1.27.51.0	73.69	T. Provini (Mondial)	8.41.8	74.44
			2 C. Ubbiali	MV	1.28.25.0	73.22			
			3 L. Taveri	MV	1.30.37.8	71.44			
	Sidecar	107½	1 F. Hillebrand	BMW	1.30.03.4	71.89	F. Hillebrand (BMW)	8.55.4	72.55
			2 W. Schneider	BMW	1.30.54.8	71.21			
			3 F. Camathias	BMW	1.32.18.2	70.14			
1958	**Senior**	264¼	1 J. Surtees	MV	2.40.39.8	98.63	J. Surtees (MV)	22.30.4	100.58
			2 R. H. F. Anderson	Norton	2.46.06.0	95.40			
			3 R. N. Brown	Norton	2.46.22.2	95.25			
	Junior	264¼	1 J. Surtees	MV	2.48.38.4	93.97	J. Surtees (MV)	23.43.4	95.42
			2 D. V. Chadwick	Norton	2.52.50.6	91.68			
			3 G. B. Tanner	Norton	2.53.06.4	91.54			
	Light-weight 250 cc	107½	1 T. Provini	MV	1.24.12.0	76.89	T. Provini (MV)	8.06.2	79.90
			2 C. Ubbiali	MV	1.24.20.2	76.77			
			3 S. M. B. Hailwood	NSU	1.27.07.8	74.30			
	Light-weight 125 cc	107½	1 C. Ubbiali	MV	1.28.51.2	72.86	C. Ubbiali (MV)	8.44.0	74.13
			2 R. Ferri	Ducati	1.29.04.4	72.68			
			3 D. V. Chadwick	Ducati	1.30.27.8	71.56			
	Sidecar	107½	1 W. Schneider	BMW	1.28.40.0	73.01	W. Schneider (BMW)	8.44.4	74.07
			2 F. Camathias	BMW	1.29.47.2	72.11			
			3 J. Beeton	Norton	1.35.34.8	67.73			
1959	**Senior**	264¼	1 J. Surtees	MV	3.00.13.4	87.94	J. Surtees (MV)	22.22.4	101.18
			2 A. King	Norton	3.05.21.0	85.00			
			3 R. Brown	Norton	3.10.56.4	83.00			
	Junior	264¼	1 J. Surtees	MV	3.00.13.4	87.94	J. Surtees (MV)	23.19.2	97.08
			2 J. Hartle	MV	2.49.12.2	93.65			
			3 A. King	Norton	2.49.22.6	93.56			
	Light-weight 250 cc	107½	1 T. Provini	MV	1.23.15.8	77.77	T. Provini (MV)	8.04.2	80.22
			2 C. Ubbiali	MV	1.23.16.2	77.76			
			3 D. Chadwick	MV	1.26.52.4	74.52			
	Light-weight 125 cc	107½	1 T. Provini	MV	1.27.25.2	74.06	L. Taveri (MZ)	8.38.0	74.99
			2 L. Taveri	MZ	1.27.32.6	73.95			
			3 S. M. B. Hailwood	Ducati	1.29.44.0	72.15			
	Sidecar	107½	1 W. Schneider	BMW	1.29.03.8	72.69	W. Schneider (BMW)	8.49.8	73.32
			2 F. Camathias	BMW	1.31.06.8	71.05			
			3 F. Scheidegger	BMW	1.33.16.2	69.42			
	Formula 1 500 cc	113¼	1 R. McIntyre	Norton	1.09.28.4	97.77	R. McIntyre (Norton)	23.01.0	98.35
			2 R. N. Brown	Norton	1.10.39.0	96.14			
			3 T. Shepherd	Norton	1.10.54.4	95.79			
	Formula 1 350 cc	113¼	1 A. King	AJS	1.11.45.4	94.66	A. King (AJS)	23.45.6	95.27
			2 R. H. F. Anderson	Norton	1.12.05.2	94.23			
			3 S. M. B. Hailwood	Norton	1.12.27.8	93.73			
1960	**Senior**	226½	1 J. Surtees	MV	2.12.35.2	102.44	J. Surtees (MV)	21.45.0	104.08
			2 J. Hartle	MV	2.15.14.2	100.44			
			3 S. M. B. Hailwood	Norton	2.18.11.6	98.29			
	Junior	226½	1 J. Hartle	MV	2.20.28.8	96.70	J. Surtees (MV)	22.49.4	99.20
			2 J. Surtees	MV	2.22.24.2	95.39			
			3 R. McIntyre	AJS	2.22.50.4	95.11			
	Light-weight 250 cc	188¾	1 G. Hocking	MV	2.00.53.0	93.64	C. Ubbiali (MV)	23.42.8	95.47
			2 C. Ubbiali	MV	2.01.33.4	93.13			
			3 T. Provini	Morini	2.01.44.6	92.98			
	Light-weight 125 cc	113¼	1 C. Ubbiali	MV	1.19.21.2	85.60	C. Ubbiali (MV)	26.17.6	86.10
			2 G. Hocking	MV	1.19.41.0	85.24			
			3 L. Taveri	MV	1.21.07.6	83.72			
	Sidecar	113¼	1 H. Fath	BMW	1.20.45.8	84.10	H. Fath (BMW)	26.23.4	85.79
			2 P. V. Harris	BMW	1.22.10.2	82.66			
			3 C. Freeman	Norton	1.28.07.2	77.08			

Year	RACE Class	Miles	Rider	Machine	Time h.m.s.	Speed mph	Fastest Lap	Time m.s.	Speed mph
1961	**Senior**	226½	1 S. M. B. Hailwood	Norton	2.15.02.0	100.60	G. Hocking	22.03.6	102.62
			2 R. McIntyre	Norton	2.16.56.4	99.20	(MV)		
			3 T. E. Phillis	Norton	2.17.31.2	98.78			
	Junior	226½	1 P. W. Read	Norton	2.22.50.0	95.10	G. Hocking	22.41.0	99.80
			2 G. Hocking	MV	2.24.07.8	94.25	(MV)		
			3 R. B. Rensen	Norton	2.25.03.0	93.65			
	Light-weight 250 cc	188¾	1 S. M. B. Hailwood	Honda	1.55.03.6	98.38	R. McIntyre	22.44.0	99.58
			2 T. E. Phillis	Honda	1.57.14.4	96.56	(Honda)		
			3 J. A. Redman	Honda	2.01.36.2	93.09			
	Light-weight 125 cc	113¼	S. M. B. Hailwood	Honda	1.16.58.6	88.23	L. Taveri	25.35.6	88.45
			2 L. Taveri	Honda	1.17.06.0	88.09	(Honda)		
			3 T. E. Phillis	Honda	1.17.49.0	87.28			
	Sidecar	113¼	1 M. Deubel	BMW	1.17.29.8	87.65	M. Deubel	25.44.0	87.97
			2 F. Scheidegger	BMW	1.18.02.6	87.03	(BMW)		
			3 P. V. Harris	BMW	1.19.40.4	85.26			
1962	**Senior**	226½	1 G. Hocking	MV	2.11.13.4	103.51	G. Hocking	21.24.4	105.75
			2 E. Boyce	Norton	2.21.06.2	96.27	(MV)		
			3 F. J. Stevens	Norton	2.21.09.4	96.24			
	Junior	226½	1 S. M. B. Hailwood	MV	2.16.24.2	99.59	S. M. B. Hailwood	22.17.2	101.58
			2 G. Hocking	MV	2.16.29.8	99.52	(MV)		
			3 F. Stastny	Jawa	2.23.23.4	94.74			
	Light-weight 250 cc	226½	1 D. W. Minter	Honda	2.20.30.0	96.68	R. McIntyre	22.51.2	99.06
			2 J. Redman	Honda	2.22.23.6	95.40	(Honda)		
			3 T. Phillis	Honda	2.26.15.6	92.87			
	Light-weight 125 cc	113½	1 L. Taveri	Honda	1.15.34.2	89.88	L. Taveri	25.07.0	90.13
			2 T. Robb	Honda	1.16.40.6	88.58	(Honda)		
			3 T. Phillis	Honda	1.16.55.0	88.30			
	50 cc	75½	1 E. Degner	Suzuki	1.00.16.4	75.12	E. Degner	29.58.6	75.52
			2 L. Taveri	Honda	1.00.34.4	74.75	(Suzuki)		
			3 T. Robb	Honda	1.00.47.6	74.48			
	Sidecar	113¼	1 C. Vincent	BSA	1.21.16.4	83.57	M. Deubel	24.57.6	90.70
			2 O. Kolle	BMW	1.21.53.8	82.93	(BMW)		
			3 C. J. Seeley	Matchless	1.22.01.8	82.90			
1963	**Senior**	226½	1 S. M. B. Hailwood	MV	2.09.48.4	104.64	S. M. B. Hailwood	21.16.4	106.41
			2 J. Hartle	Gilera	2.11.01.8	103.67	(MV)		
			3 P. W. Read	Gilera	2.15.42.2	100.10			
	Junior	226½	1 J. A. Redman	Honda	2.23.08.2	94.91	J. A. Redman	22.20.8	101.30
			2 J. Hartle	Gilera	2.29.58.2	90.58	(Honda)		
			3 F. Stastny	Jawa	2.31.20.6	89.76			
	Light-weight 250 cc	226½	1 J. A. Redman	Honda	2.23.13.2	94.85	J. A. Redman	23.17.0	97.23
			2 F. Ito	Yamaha	2.23.40.4	94.55	(Honda)		
			3 W. A. Smith	Honda	2.29.05.2	91.12			
	Light-weight 125 cc	113¼	1 H. R. Anderson	Suzuki	1.16.05.0	89.27	H. R. Anderson	24.47.4	91.32
			2 F. G. Perris	Suzuki	1.17.25.0	87.74	(Suzuki)		
			3 E. Degner	Suzuki	1.17.31.6	87.61			
	50 cc	113¼	1 M. Itch	Suzuki	1.26.10.6	78.81	E. Degner	28.37.2	79.10
			2 H. R. Anderson	Suzuki	1.26.37.4	78.40	(Suzuki)		
			3 H. G. Anscheidt	Kreidler	1.26.42.0	78.33			
	Sidecar	113¼	1 F. Camathias	FCS	1.16.51.0	88.38	F. Camathias	25.19.0	89.42
			2 F. Scheidegger	BMW	1.17.29.2	87.66	(FCS)		
			3 A. Birch	BMW	1.21.17.6	83.52			
1964	**Senior**	226½	1 S. M. B. Hailwood	MV	2.14.33.8	100.95	S. M. B. Hailwood	22.05.0	102.51
			2 D. Minter	Norton	2.17.56.6	98.47	(MV)		
			3 F. Stevens	Matchless	2.20.54.6	96.40			
	Junior	226½	1 J. Redman	Honda	2.17.55.4	98.50	J. Redman	22.28.0	100.76
			2 P. W. Read	AJS	2.25.09.6	93.58	(Honda)		
			3 M. A. Duff	AJS	2.25.21.4	93.46			
	Light-weight 250 cc	226½	1 J. Redman	Honda	2.19.23.6	97.45	P. W. Read	22.46.2	99.42
			2 A. Shepherd	MZ	2.20.04.6	96.67	(Yamaha)		
			3 A. Pagani	Paton	2.37.35.8	86.20			

Year	RACE Class	Miles	Rider	Machine	Time h.m.s.	Speed mph	Fastest Lap	Time m.s.	Speed mph
1964	**Light-weight 125 cc**	113¼	1 L. Taveri 2 J. Redman 3 R. Bryans	Honda Honda Honda	1.13.43.0 1.13.46.0 1.14.28.2	92.14 92.08 91.22	L. Taveri (Honda)	24.12.2	93.53
	50 cc	113¼	1 H. R. Anderson 2 R. Bryans 3 I. Morishita	Suzuki Honda Suzuki	1.24.13.4 1.25.14.8 1.25.15.4	80.64 79.68 79.67	H. R. Anderson (Suzuki)	27.54.2	81.13
	Sidecar	113¼	1 M. Deubel 2 C. Seeley 3 G. Auerbacher	BMW FCSB BMW	1.16.13.0 1.18.17.6 1.20.26.2	89.12 86.76 84.45	M. Deubel (BMW)	25.15.4	89.63
1965	**Senior**	226½	1 S.M.B. Hailwood 2 J. Dunphy 3 M. Duff	MV Norton Matchless	2.28.09.0 2.30.28.8 2.34.12.0	91.69 90.28 88.09	S. M.B. Hailwood (MV)	23.48.2	95.11
	Junior	226½	1 J. Redman 2 P. W. Read 3 G. Agostini	Honda Yamaha MV	2.14.52.2 2.16.44.4 2.17.53.4	100.72 99.35 98.52	S. M. B. Hailwood (MV)	22.00.6	102.85
	Light-weight 250 cc	226½	1 J. Redman 2 M. Duff 3 F. Perris	Honda Yamaha Suzuki	2.19.45.8 2.23.26.4 2.24.32.0	97.19 94.71 93.99	J. Redman (Honda)	22.37.0	100.09
	Light-weight 125 cc	113¼	1 P. W. Read 2 L. Taveri 3 M. Duff	Yamaha Honda Yamaha	1.12.02.6 1.12.08.4 1.12.23.6	94.28 94.15 93.83	H. R. Anderson (Suzuki)	23.34.6	96.02
	50 cc	113¼	1 L. Taveri 2 H. R. Anderson 3 E. Degner	Honda Suzuki Suzuki	1.25.15.6 1.26.08.8 1.28.10.0	79.66 78.85 77.04	L. Taveri (Honda)	28.00.4	80.83
	Sidecar	113¼	1 M. Deubel 2 F. Scheidegger 3 G. Auerbacher	BMW BMW BMW	1.14.59.8 1.15.13.8 1.20.26.2	90.57 90.11 84.45	M. Deubel (BMW)	24.39.6	91.80
1966	**Senior**	226½	1 S. M. B. Hailwood 2 G. Agostini 3 C. R. Conn	Honda MV Norton	2.11.44.8 2.14.22.6 2.22.26.8	103.11 101.09 95.37	S. M. B. Hailwood (Honda)	21.08.06	107.07
	Junior	226½	1 G. Agostini 2 P. J. Williams 3 C. R. Conn	MV AJS Norton	2.14.40.4 2.24.46.6 2.26.45.4	100.87 93.83 92.56	G. Agostini (MV)	21.57.6	103.09
	Light-weight 250 cc	226½	1 S. M. B. Hailwood 2 S. Graham 3 P. G. Inchley	Honda Honda Villiers	2.13.26.0 2.19.20.0 2.28.34.4	101.79 97.49 91.43	S. M. B. Hailwood (Honda)	21.42.4	104.29
	Light-weight 125 cc	113¼	1 W. Ivy 2 P. W. Read 3 H. R. Anderson	Yamaha Yamaha Suzuki	1.09.32.8 1.10.03.2 1.10.09.2	97.66 96.96 96.82	W. Ivy (Yamaha)	22.58.2	98.55
	50 cc	113¼	1 R. Bryans 2 L. Taveri 3 H. R. Anderson	Honda Honda Suzuki	1.19.17.2 1.20.08.4 1.21.41.0	85.66 84.74 83.14	R. Bryans (Honda)	26.10.2	85.66
	Sidecar	113¼	1 F. Scheidegger 2 M. Deubel 3 G. Auerbacher	BMW BMW BMW	1.14.50.0 1.14.50.8 1.16.52.4	90.76 90.75 88.35	M. Deubel (BMW)	24.42.4	91.63
1967	**Senior**	226.4	1 S. M. B. Hailwood 2 P. J. Williams 3 S. Spencer	Honda Arter Matchless Lancefield Norton	2.08.36.2 2.16.20.0 2.17.47.2	105.62 99.64 98.59	S. M. B. Hailwood (Honda)	20.48.8	108.77
	Junior	226.4	1 S. M. B. Hailwood 2 G. Agostini 3 D. Woodman	Honda MV Agusta MZ	2.09.45.6 2.12.48.8 2.20.53.6	104.68 102.28 96.41	S. M. B. Hailwood (Honda)	21.00.8	107.73
	Light-weight 250 cc	226.4	1 S. M. B. Hailwood 2 P. W. Read 3 R. Bryans	Honda Yamaha Honda	2.11.47.6 2.13.06.4 2.16.27	103.07 102.05 99.55	S. M. B. Hailwood (Honda)	21.39.8	104.50
	Light-weight 125 cc	113.2	1 P. W. Read 2 S. Graham 3 A. Motohashi	Yamaha Suzuki Yamaha	1.09.40.8 1.09.44.2 1.11.49.6	97.48 97.40 94.56	P. W. Read (Yamaha)	23.00.8	98.36
	50 cc	113.2	1 S. Graham 2 H. G. Anscheidt 3 T. Robb	Suzuki Suzuki Suzuki	1.21.56.8 1.22.58.0 1.38.02.0	82.89 81.86 69.28	S. Graham (Suzuki)	26.34.4	85.19

Year	RACE Class	Miles	Rider	Machine	Time h.m.s.	Speed mph	Fastest Lap	Time m.s.	Speed mph
1967	**Production 750 cc**	113.2	1 J. Hartle	Triumph Bonneville	1.09.56.8	97.10	J. Hartle	23.07.8	97.87
			2 P. Smart	Dunstall Dominator	1.11.48.0	94.60	(Triumph Bonneville)		
			3 A. J. Smith	BSA Spitfire	1.15.42.0	89.73			
	Production 500 cc	113.2	1 N. Kelly	Velo Thruxton Venom	1.15.33.8	89.89	N. Kelly	24.52.6	91.01
			2 K. Heckles	Velo Thruxton Venom	1.16.11.6	89.15	(Velo Thruxton		
			3 D. J. Nixon	Triumph T100	1.19.48.0	85.11	Venom)		
	Production 250 cc	113.2	1 W. A. Smith	Bultaco Metralla	1.16.38.2	88.63	W. A. Smith	25.19.4	89.41
			2 T. Robb	Bultaco Metralla	1.16.38.6	88.62	(Bultaco Metralla)		
			3 B. Smith	Suzuki	1.18.43.2	86.29			
	Sidecar 500 cc	113.2	1 S. Schauzu	BMW	1.14.40.6	90.96	G. Auerbacher	24.41.2	91.70
			2 K. Enders	BMW	1.14.59.2	90.58	(BMW)		
			3 C. Seeley	BMW	1.17.15.6	87.92			
1968	**Senior**	226.4	1 G. Agostini	MV Agusta	2.13.39.4	101.63	G. Agostini	21.34.8	104.91
			2 B. A. Ball	Seeley	2.22.08.4	95.57	(MV Agusta)		
			3 B. J. Randle	Petty-Norton	2.22.08.8	95.56			
	Junior	226.4	1 G. Agostini	MV Agusta	2.09.38.6	104.78	G. Agostini	21.12.2	106.77
			2 R. Pasolini	Benelli	2.12.19.6	102.65	(MV Agusta)		
			3 W. A. Smith	Honda	2.22.58.6	95.02			
	Light-weight 250 cc	226.4	1 W. D. Ivy	Yamaha	2.16.24.8	99.58	W. D. Ivy	21.27.4	105.51
			2 R. Pasolini	Benelli	2.18.36.8	98.00	(Yamaha)		
			3 H. Rosner	MZ	2.22.56.4	95.04			
	Light-weight 125 cc	113.2	1 P. W. Read	Yamaha	1.08.31.4	99.12	W. D. Ivy	22.34.0	100.32
			2 W. D. Ivy	Yamaha	1.09.27.8	97.78	(Yamaha)		
			3 K. Carruthers	Gates Honda	1.18.21.2	86.69			
	50 cc	113.2	1 B. Smith	Derbi	1.33.10.4	72.90	B. Smith	30.46.0	73.44
			2 C. M. Walpole	Honda	1.40.59.6	67.26	(Derbi)		
			3 E. L. Griffiths	Honda	1.42.36.0	66.20			
	Production 750 cc	113.2	1 R. Pickrell	Dunstall Dominator	1.09.13.2	98.13	R. Pickrell	22.46.6	99.39
			2 B. Nelson	Norton Atlas	1.11.47.2	94.62	(Dunstall Dominator)		
			3 A. J. Smith	BSA Spitfire	1.12.23.8	93.82			
	Production 500 cc	113.2	1 R. Knight	Triumph Daytona	1.15.23.6	90.09	R. L. Knight	24.52.2	91.03
			2 J. Blanchard	Velocette Thruxton	1.16.41.2	88.58	(Triumph Daytona)		
			3 D. J. Nixon	Triumph Daytona	1.16.44.4	88.52			
	Production 250 cc	113.2	1 T. E. Burgess	Ossa	1.17.53.4	87.21	T. E. Burgess	25.45.4	87.89
			2 G. E. Leigh	Bultaco Metralla	1.19.41.8	85.23	(Ossa)		
			3 B. Smith	Thompson Suzuki	1.19.45.0	85.17			
	Sidecar 500 cc	113.2	1 S. Schauzu	BMW	1.14.34.2	91.09	K. Enders	24.00.0	94.32
			2 J. Attenberger	BMW	1.15.55.2	89.47	(BMW)		
			3 H. Luthringshauser	BMW	1.17.32.6	87.60			
	Sidecar 750 cc	113.2	1 T. Vinicombe	Kirby-BSA	1.19.07.4	85.85	C. Vincent	25.25.0	89.11
			2 N. Hanks	BSA	1.21.44.0	83.10	(BSA)		
			3 P. Brown	BSA	1.21.48.0	83.03			
1969	**Senior**	226.4	1 G. Agostini	MV	2.09.40.2	104.75	G. Agostini	21.18.4	106.25
			2 A. J. Barnett	Kirby-Metisse	2.18.12.6	98.28	(MV)		
			3 T. Dickie	Kuhn-Seeley	2.18.44.2	97.92			
	Junior	226.4	1 G. Agostini	MV Agusta	2.13.25.4	101.81	G. Agostini	21.46.0	104.00
			2 B. Steenson	Aermacchi	2.23.36.4	94.60	(MV)		
			3 J. Findlay	Beart-Aermacchi	2.24.41.2	93.89			
	Light-weight 250 cc	226.4	1 K. Carruthers	Benelli	2.21.35.2	95.95	K. Carruthers	22.51.8	99.01
			2 F. Perris	Crooks Suzuki	2.24.59.4	93.69	(Benelli)		
			3 S. Herrero	Ossa	2.26.21.0	92.82			
	Light-weight 125 cc	113.2	1 D. A. Simmonds	Kawasaki	1.14.34.6	91.08	D. A. Simmonds	24.29.0	92.46
			2 K. Carruthers	Aermacchi	1.20.27.2	84.43	(Kawasaki)		
			3 R. J. G. Dickinson	Honda	1.21.10.6	83.67			
	Production 750 cc	113.2	1 M. Uphill	Triumph Bonneville	1.07.55.4	99.99	M. Uphill	22.33.2	100.37
			2 P. Smart	Norton Commando	1.08.21.2	99.37	(Triumph Bonneville)		
			3 D. Pendlebury	Triumph Bonneville	1.10.16.2	96.66			
	Production 500 cc	113.2	1 W. G. Penny	Honda CB450	1.17.01.6	88.18	T. Dunnell	24.55.2	90.84
			2 R. L. Knight	Triumph Daytona	1.17.30.4	87.64	(Kawasaki		
			3 R. W. Baylie	Triumph Daytona	1.19.04.0	85.90	Mach 3)		

Year	RACE Class	Miles	Rider	Machine	Time h.m.s.	Speed mph	Fastest Lap	Time m.s.	Speed mph
1969	**Production 250 cc**	113.2	1 A. M. Rogers 2 F. Whiteway 3 C. S. Mortimer	Ducati Mach 1 Suzuki T20 Ducati Mach 3	1.21.03.8 1.21.33.4 1.22.49.6	83.79 83.29 82.01	C. S. Mortimer (Ducati Mach 3)	26.35.6	85.13
	Sidecar 500 cc	113.2	1 K. Enders 2 S. Schauzu 3 H. Fath	BMW BMW URS	1.13.27.0 1.14.39.4 1.15.00.0	92.48 90.99 90.56	K. Enders (BMW)	24.27.8	92.54
	Sidecar 750 cc	113.2	1 S. Schauzu 2 P. M. Brown 3 L.W.Currie	BMW BSA LWC	1.15.36.8 1.19.18.2 1.23.07.4	89.83 85.65 81.72	S. Schauzu (BMW)	24.35.4	92.06
1970	**Senior**	226.4	1 G. Agostini 2 P. J. Williams 3 W. A. Smith	MV Arter Matchless Kawasaki	2.13.47.6 2.18.57.0 2.21.07.6	101.52 97.76 96.26	G. Agostini (MV)	21.30.0	105.29
	Junior	226.4	1 G. Agostini 2 A. J. Barnett 3 P. Smart	MV Aermacchi Padgett-Yamaha	2.13.28.6 2.18.23.8 2.20.08.8	101.77 98.16 96.93	G. Agostini (MV)	21.39.0	104.56
	Light-weight 250 cc	226.4	1 K. Carruthers 2 R. Gould 3 G. Bartusch	Yamaha Yamaha MZ	2.21.19.2 2.24.54.0 2.26.58.4	96.13 93.75 92.43	K. Carruthers (Yamaha)	23.05.4	98.04
	Light-weight 125 cc	113.2	1 D. Braun 2 B. Jansson 3 G. Bartusch	Suzuki Maico MZ	1.16.05.0 1.18.28.4 1.19.02.8	89.27 86.56 85.93	D. A. Simmonds (Kawasaki)	24.52.2	90.90
	Production 750 cc	188.65	1 M. Uphill 2 P. J. Williams 3 R. Pickrel	Triumph Trident Norton Commando Norton Commando	1.55.51.0 1.53.52.6 1.58.05.2	97.71 97.69 95.86	P. J. Williams (Norton Commando)	22.38.4	99.99
	Production 500 cc	188.65	1 F. Whiteway 2 G. Pantall 3 R. L. Knight	Suzuki T500 II Triumph Daytona Triumph Daytona	2.05.52.0 2.07.20.0 2.07.20.4	89.94 88.90 88.89	F. Whiteway (Suzuki T500 II)	24.57.0	90.75
	Production 250 cc	188.65	1 C. Mortimer 2 J. Williams 3 S. Woods	Ducati Mk III Honda CB250 Suzuki T250	2.13.23.4 2.13.29.0 2.14.40.6	84.87 84.80 84.06	C. Mortimer (Ducati Mk III)	26.25.6	86.71
	Sidecar 500 cc	113.2	1 K. Enders 2 S. Schauzu 3 H. Luthringshauser	BMW BMW BMW	1.13.05.6 1.14.56.4 1.16.58.0	92.93 90.64 88.25	K. Enders (BMW)	24.08.2	93.79
	Sidecar 750 cc	113.2	1 S. Schauzu 2 P. Brown 3 E. Leece	BMW BSA LMS	1.15.18.0 1.19.00.4 1.23.50.2	90.20 85.97 81.02	K. Enders (BMW)	24.30.6	92.37
1971	**Senior**	226.4	1 G. Agostini 2 P. J. Williams 3 F. Perris	MV Arter Matchless Suzuki	2.12.24.4 2.18.03.0 2.20.45.4	102.59 98.40 96.51	G. Agostin (MV)	21.35.4	104.86
	Junior	188.65	1 A. Jefferies 2 G. Pantall 3 W. A. Smith	Yamsel Padgett Yamaha Honda	2.05.48.6 2.06.25.0 2.07.04.8	89.98 89.55 89.09	P. Read (Yamaha)	22.33.2	100.37
	Light-weight 250 cc	150.92	1 P. Read 2 B. Randle 3 A. J. Barnett	Yamaha Yamaha Yamsel	1.32.23.6 1.34.27.6 1.35.02.0	98.02 95.87 95.29	P. Read (Yamaha)	22.37.2	100.08
	Light-weight 125 cc	113.19	1 C. Mortimer 2 B. Jansson 3 J. Kiddie	Yamaha Maico Honda	1.20.54.0 1.23.43.6 1.29.12.2	83.96 81.13 77.14	C. Mortimer (Yamaha)	26.00.2	87.05
	Formula 750 cc	113.19	1 A. Jefferies 2 R. Pickrell 3 P. J. Williams	750 cc Triumph 750 cc BSA 750 cc Norton	1.06.02.0 1.06.28.0 1.07.06.2	102.85 102.18 101.22	A. Jefferies (750 cc Triumph)	21.56.0	103.21
	Production 750 cc	150.92	1 R. Pickrel 2 A. Jefferies 3 R. Heath	Triumph Trident Triumph Trident BSA Rocket 3	1.30.30.2 1.32.03.0 1.33.17.4	100.07 98.38 97.08	P. Williams	22.24.0	101.06
	Production 500 cc	150.02	1 J. Williams 2 G. Penny 3 A. Cooper	Honda CB 450 Honda CB 450 Suzuki T500	1.39.28.8 1.41.39.6 1.44.32.8	91.04 89.09 86.63	J. Williams	24.45.4	91.45
	Production 250 cc	150.92	1 W. A. Smith 2 C. Willaims 3 T. Robb	Honda CB 250 Yamaha YDS 7 Honda CB 250	1.47.43.6 1.47.52.0 1.49.47.6	84.14 84.04 82.49	C. Williams Yamaha YDS 7	26.44.8	84.64

Year	RACE Class	Miles	Rider	Machine	Time h.m.s.	Speed mph	Fastest Lap	Time m.s.	Speed mph
1971	**Sidecar 500 cc**	113.19	1 S. Schauzu	BMW	1.19.47.8	86.21	G. Auerbacher	25.56.2	87.27
			2 G. Auberbacher	BMW	1.18.53.2	86.10	(BMW)		
			3 A. Butscher	BMW	1.23.32.6	81.31			
	Sidecar 750 cc	113.19	1 G. Auerbacher	BMW	1.18.12.0	86.86	S. Schauzu	24.13.6	93.44
			2 A. J. Sansum	Triumph	1.22.20.2	82.50	(BMW)		
			3 R. Williamson	WHB Weslake	1.22.35.0	82.25			
1972	**Senior**	226.38	1 G. Agostini	MV	2.10.34.4	104.02	G. Agostini	21.28.8	105.39
			2 A. Pagani	MV	2.18.25.8	98.13	(MV)		
			3 M. Grant	Yamaha	2.20.00.0	97.03			
	Junior	188.65	1 G. Agostini	MV	1.50.56.8	102.03	G. Agostini	21.54.4	103.34
			2 T. Rutter	Yamaha	1.55.21.4	98.13	(MV)		
			3 M. Grant	Yamaha	1.56.01.0	97.57			
	Light-weight 250 cc	150.92	1 P. W. Read	Yamaha	1.30.51.2	99.68	P. W. Read	22.30.0	100.61
			2 R. Gould	Yamaha	1.32.10.6	98.09	(Yamaha)		
			3 J. Williams	Yamaha	1.33.16.4	97.09			
	Light-weight 125 cc	113.19	1 C. Mortimer	Yamaha	1.17.38.2	87.49	C. Mortimer	24.59.6	90.58
			2 C. Williams	Yamaha	1.24.23.0	80.49	(Yamaha)		
			3 W. Rae	Maico	1.25.39.8	79.29			
	Formula 750 cc	188.65	1 R. Pickrell	Triumph	1.48.36.0	104.23	R. Pickrell	21.25.2	105.68
			2 A. Jefferies	Triumph	1.49.28.4	103.46	(Triumph)		
			3 J. Findlay	Suzuki	1.55.07.4	98.33			
	Production 750 cc	150.92	1 R. Pickrell	Triumph	1.30.34.0	100.00	R. Pickrell	22.16.8	101.61
			2 P. J. Williams	Norton	1.33.48.8	96.53	(Triumph)		
			3 D. Nixon	Triumph	1.36.18.4	94.04			
	Production 500 cc	150.92	1 S. Woods	Suzuki	1.38.13.3	92.20	S. Woods	24.11.0	93.61
			2 R. Bowler	Triumph	1.38.20.6	92.09	(Suzuki)		
			3 W. A. Smith	Honda	1.46.08.8	91.16			
	Production 250 cc	150.92	1 J. Williams	Honda	1.46.08.8	85.32	J. Williams	26.24.4	85.73
			2 C. Williams	Yamaha	1.47.50.2	84.06	(Honda)		
			3 E. Roberts	Suzuki	1.48.56.4	83.14			
	Sidecar 500 cc	113.19	1 S. Schauzu	BMW	1.13.57.2	91.85	H. Luthringshauser	24.28.0	92.53
			2 H. Luthringshauser	BMW	1.14.04.6	91.70	(BMW)		
			3 G. Boret	Konig	1.20.27.4	84.43			
	Sidecar 750 cc	113.19	1 S. Schauzu	BMW	1.14.40.0	90.97	S. Schauzu	24.47.2	91.33
			2 A. J. Sansum	Triumph	1.17.24.0	87.76	(BMW)		
			3 J. L. Barker	BSA	1.18.41.6	86.32			
1973	**Senior**	226½	1 J. Findlay	Suzuki	2.13.45.2	101.55	M. Grant	21.40.8	104.41
			2 P. J. Williams	Matchless	2.14.59.4	100.62	(Yamaha)		
			3 C. Sanby	Suzuki	2.15.27.6	100.27			
	Junior	188¾	1 T. Rutter	Yamaha	1.50.58.8	101.99	T. Rutter	21.43.2	104.22
			2 K. Huggett	Yamaha	1.52.31.6	100.58	(Yamaha)		
			3 J. Williams	Yamaha	1.52.49.4	100.32			
	Light-weight 250 cc	151	1 C. Williams	Yamaha	1.30.30	100.05	C. Williams	22.8.4	102.24
			2 J. Williams	Yamaha	1.30.54.6	99.60	(Yamaha)		
			3 W. Rae	Yamaha	1.31.35.4	98.86			
	Light-weight 125 cc	113¼	1 T. Robb	Yamaha	1.16.23.6	88.90	S. Woods	25.22	89.24
			2 J. Kostwinder	Yamaha	1.17.21.6	87.79	(Suzuki)		
			3 N. Tuxworth	Yamaha	1.18.27.2	86.56			
	Formula 750 cc	188¾	1 P. J. Williams	Norton	1.47.19.2	105.47	E. Roberts	21.6.2	107.27
			2 M. Grant	Norton	1.50.21.6	102.56	(Yamaha)		
			3 A. Jefferies	Triumph	1.50.55.2	102.04			
	Production 750 cc	151	1 A. Jefferies	Triumph	1.34.41.6	95.62	T. Robb	22.31.2	100.52
			2 J. Williams	Triumph	1.35.24.8	94.90	(Danfay Yamaha)		
			3 D. Nixon	Triumph	1.38.53.6	91.56			
	Production 500 cc	151	1 W. Smith	Honda	1.42.47	88.10	P. J. Williams	23.58.2	94.44
			2 S. Woods	Suzuki	1.42.55.2	87.98	(Norton)		
			3 K. Martin	Kawasaki	1.43.2.8	87.87			
	Production 250 cc	151	1 C. Williams	Yamaha	1.50.45	81.76	P. J. Williams	26.55.8	84.06
			2 E. Roberts	Yamaha	1.51.27	81.24	(Norton)		
			3 T. Robb	Honda	1.53.5.8	80.06			

Year	RACE Class	Miles	Rider	Machine	Time h.m.s.	Speed mph	Fastest Lap	Time m.s.	Speed mph
1973	**Sidecar**	113¼	1 K. Enders	BMW	1.11.32.4	94.93	K. Enders	23.46.4	95.25
	500 cc		2 S. Schauzu	BMW	1.14.18.2	91.40	(BMW)		
			3 R. Steinhausen	Konig	1.15.35.4	89.94			
	Sidecar	113¼	1 K. Enders	BMW	1.13.1	93.01	K. Enders	23.22.2	96.86
	750 cc		2 S. Schauzu	BMW	1.14.2.4	91.72	(BMW)		
			3 J. Brandon	Honda	1.20.8	84.75			
1974	**Senior**	188¾	1 P. Carpenter	Yamaha	1.56.41.6	96.99	C. Williams	22.12.6	101.92
			2 C. Williams	Yamaha	1.57.31.6	96.31	(Yamaha)		
			3 T. Rutter	Yamaha	1.59.57.4	94.35			
	Junior	188¾	1 T. Rutter	Yamaha	1.48.22.2	104.44	C. Mortimer	21.16.6	106.39
			2 M. Grant	Yamaha	1.50.6.2	102.80	(Yamaha)		
			3 P. Cott	Yamaha	1.51.47	101.25			
	Light-	151	1 C. Williams	Yamaha	1.36.9.8	94.16	M. Grant	23.8	97.85
	weight		2 M. Grant	Yamaha	1.37.9.2	93.20	Yamaha)		
	250 cc		3 C. Mortimer	Yamaha	1.37.31.2	92.85			
	Light-	113¼	1 C. Horton	Yamaha	1.16.47	88.44	A. Hockley	25.29.8	88.78
	weight		2 I. Hodgkinson	Yamaha	1.17.27	87.68	(Yamaha)		
	125 cc		3 T. Herron	Yamaha	1.18.8.6	86.91			
	Formula	262½	1 C. Mortimer	Yamaha	2.15.7.2	100.52	C. Williams	21.14	106.61
	750 cc		2 C. Williams	Yamaha	2.15.15.8	100.41	(Yamaha)		
			3 T. Rutter	Yamaha	2.15.42.6	100.08			
	Production	151	1 M. Grant	Triumph	1.30.48	99.72	M. Grant	22.28.2	100.74
	1000 cc		2 H. O. Butenuth	BMW	1.32.41	97.70	(Triumph)		
			3 H. Dahne	BMW	1.33.20.6	97.01			
	Production	151	1 K. Martin	Kawasaki	1.36.28.6	93.85	K. Martin	23.46.6	95.21
	500 cc		2 A. Rogers	Triumph	1.36.58	93.38	(Kawasaki)		
			3 P. Gurner	BSA	1.38.14.4	92.17			
	Production	151	1 M. Sharpe	Yamaha	1.44.9.2	86.94	E. Roberts	25.35	88.48
	250 cc		2 E. Roberts	Yamaha	1.44.11.6	86.90	(Yamaha)		
			3 B. Rae	Suzuki	1.45.22.6	85.93			
	Sidecar	113¼	1 H. Luthringshauser	Yamaha	1.13.36.2	92.27	J. Gawley	24.14.8	93.36
	500 cc		2 G. O'Dell	Yamaha	1.18.46.4	86.21	(Konig)		
			3 M. Hobson	Yamaha	1.19.35	85.33			
	Sidecar	113¼	1 S. Schauzu	BMW	1.10.18.4	96.59	R. Steinhausen	23.3.4	98.18
	750 cc		2 H. Luthringshauser	BMW	1.13.52.2	91.93	(Konig)		
			3 M. Horspole	Weslake	1.16.30.6	88.76			
1975	**Senior**	226.38	1 M. Grant	Kawasaki	2.15.27.6	100.27	M. Grant	21.59.6	102.93
			2 J. Williams	Yamaha	2.15.58.8	99.88	(Kawasaki)		
			3 C. Mortimer	Yamaha	2.18.22.8	98.15			
	Junior	188.65	1 C. Williams	Yamaha	1.48.26.4	104.38	A. George	21.17.8	106.29
			2 C. Mortimer	Yamaha	1.49.51.0	103.04	(Yamaha)		
			3 T. Herron	Yamaha	1.50.35.4	102.35			
	Light-	150.92	1 C. Mortimer	Yamaha	1.28.57.8	101.78	D. Chatterton	21.59.4	103.54
	weight		2 D. Chatterton	Yamaha	1.28.20.0	101.36	(Yamaha)		
	250 cc		3 J. Williams	Yamaha	1.29.42.2	100.94			
	Classic	226.38	1 J. Williams	Yamaha	2.08.56.8	105.33	M. Grant	20.36.8	109.82
	1000 cc		2 P. Tait	Yamaha	2.12.54.4	102.19	(Kawasaki)		
			3 C. Sanby	Suzuki	2.13.28.4	101.76			
	Production	377.3	1 D. Croxford/	Triumph	4.01.17.2	99.60	D. Croxford/	22.01.0	102.82
	1000 cc		A. George				A. George		
			2 S. Griffiths/	Triumph	4.06.04.4	97.54	(Triumph)		
			D. Williams						
			3 M. Sharpe/	BMW	4.10.06.4	95.88			
			A. Alexander						
	Production	377.3	1 C. Williams/	Honda	4.11.18.2	90.08	P. Gurner/	23.39.9	95.65
	500cc		E. Roberts				D. Saville		
			2 C. Revett	Honda	4.12.58.8	89.48	(BSA)		
			S. Parrish						
			3 N. Tuxworth/	Honda	4.13.15.2	89.38			
			C. Horton						

Year	RACE Class	Miles	Rider	Time Machine	Speed h.m.s.	Fastest mph	Time Lap	Speed m.s.	mph
1975	**Production 250 cc**	377.3	1 C. Mortimer/ B. Guthrie	Yamaha	4.03.42.6	86.43	C. Mortimer/ B. Guthrie (Yamaha)	25.36.0	88.43
			2 S. Jones/ W. Simpson	Yamaha	4.07.35.6	85.03			
			3 A. North/ M. Patrick	Yamaha	4.08.30.6	84.71			
	Sidecar 500 cc	113.19	1 R. Steinhausen	Konig	1.10.47.0	95.94	M. Hobson (Yamaha)	23.24.4	96.71
			2 M. Hobson	Yamaha	1.10.51.0	95.85			
			3 D. Greasley	Yamaha	1.12.04.6	94.22			
	Sidecar 1000 cc	113.19	1 S. Schauzu	BMW	1.09.37.0	97.55	S. Schauzu (BMW)	22.47.6	99.31
			2 D. Greasley	Yamaha	1.10.33.0	96.26			
			3 G. Boret	Konig	1.13.30.6	92.38			
1976	**Senior**	226.38	1 T. Herron	Yamaha	2.09.10.0	105.15	J. Williams (Suzuki)	20.09.8	112.27
			2 I. Richards	Yamaha	2.09.13.4	105.11			
			3 B. Guthrie	Yamaha	2.09.33.0	104.84			
	Junior	188.65	1 C. Mortimer	Yamaha	1.46.00.2	106.78	T. Rutter (Yamaha)	20.49.6	108.69
			2 T. Rutter	Yamaha	1.47.07.0	106.66			
			3 B. Guthrie	Yamaha	1.49.01.8	103.81			
	Light-weight 250 cc	150.92	1 T. Herron	Yamaha	1.27.26.8	103.55	T. Herron (Yamaha)	21.27.8	105.47
			2 T. Katayama	Yamaha	1.27.52.2	103.05			
			3 C. Mortimer	Yamaha	1.28.43.2	102.06			
	Open Classic	226.38	1 J. Williams	Suzuki	2.05.33.0	108.18	J. Williams (Suzuki)	20.32.4	110.21
			2 A. George	Yamaha	2.06.57.8	106.98			
			3 T. Rutter	Yamaha	2.08.19.6	105.84			
	Production 1000 cc	377.30	1 H. Dahne/ O. Butenuth	BMW	4.08.50.8	98.92	S. Tonkin/ R. Nicholls (Ducati)	21.57.0	103.13
			2 M. Sharpe/ A. Alexander	BMW	4.17.00.4	95.50			
			3 R. Knight/ M. Hunt	Laverda	4.19.36.0	94.48			
	Production 500 cc	377.30	1 F. Rutter/ M. Poxon	Honda	4.08.15.4	91.98	I. Richards (Suzuki)	23.43.0	95.45
			2 J. Kidson/ B. Henderson	Honda	4.08.48.2	90.98			
			3 N. Rollason/ L. Trotter	Suzuki	4.11.38.2	89.96			
	Production 250 cc	377.30	1 C. Mortimer/ B. Simpson	Yamaha	4.05.09.8	87.00	C. Mortimer/ B. Simpson (Yamaha)	25.17.2	89.52
			2 T. Rutter/ D. Hughes	Suzuki	4.06.37.8	86.46			
			3 K. Martin/ J. Riley	Yamaha	4.10.55.4	84.91			
	Sidecar 500 cc	113.19	1 R. Steinhausen	Konig	1.10.26.0	96.42	S. Schauzu/ W. Kalauch	23.10.0	97.50
			2 D. Greasley	Yamaha	1.10.59.8	95.65			
			3 M. Hobson	Yamaha	1.11.09.6	95.43			
	Sidecar 1000 cc	113.19	1 M. Hobson	Yamaha	1.09.27.8	97.77	M. Hobson (Yamaha)	22.38.8	99.96
			2 S. Schauzu	BMW	1.10.12.4	96.73			
			3 D. Greasley	Yamaha	1.10.50.0	95.86			
1977	**500 cc**	188.65	1 P. Read	Suzuki	1.45.48.4	106.97	P. Read (Suzuki)	20.34.6	110.01
			2 T. Herron	Yamaha	1.47.06.6	105.67			
			3 E. Roberts	Yamaha	1.48.34.4	104.25			
	250 cc	113.19	1 C. Williams	Yamaha	1.08.10.0	99.62	I. Richards (Yamaha)	22.18.8	101.45
			2 I. Richards	Yamaha	1.08.18.8	99.41			
			3 T. Herron	Yamaha	1.09.23.0	97.88			
	Classic	226.38	1 M. Grant	Kawasaki	2.02.37.4	110.76	M. Grant (Kawasaki)	20.04.4	112.77
			2 C. Williams	Yamaha	2.06.04.2	107.74			
			3 E. Roberts	Yamaha	2.08.03.0	106.07			
	Jubilee TT	150.29	1 J. Dunlop	Yamaha	1.23.10.6	108.86	J. Dunlop (Yamaha)	20.24.4	110.93
			2 G. Fogarty	Suzuki	1.24.02.2	107.75			
			3 S. Tonkin	Yamaha	1.24.31.0	107.14			
	Formula One	150.92	1 P. Read	Honda	1.33.19.6	97.02	P. Read (Honda)	22.15.0	101.74
			2 R. Nicholls	Ducati	1.33.58.0	96.36			
			3 I. Richards	Honda	1.34.46.0	95.55			

Year	RACE Class	Miles	Rider	Time Machine	Speed h.m.s.	Fastest mph	Time Lap	Speed m.s.	mph
1977	**Formula Two**	150.92	1 A. Jackson	Honda	1.31.08.0	99.36	A. Jackson (Honda)	22.22.8	101.15
			2 N. Tuxworth	Honda	1.32.32.6	97.84			
			3 D. Casement	Honda	1.34.58.4	95.34			
	Formula Three	159.92	1 J. Kidson	Honda	1.37.04.4	93.28	J. Kidson (Honda)	23.52.6	94.81
			2 D. Loan	Suzuki	1.38.04.4	92.33			
			3 B. Peters	Suzuki	1.42.19.4	88.49			
	Sidecar 500 cc	150.21	1 G. O'Dell/ K. Arthur	Yamaha	1.30.31.2	100.30	G. O'Dell/ K. Arthur (Yamaha)	22.01.2	102.80
			2 D. Greasley/ M. Skeels	Yamaha	1.31.21.2	99.12			
			3 R. Steinhausen/ W. Kalauch	Konig	1.32.17.4	98.11			
	Sidecar 1000 cc	150.29	1 M. Hobson/ S. Collins	Yamaha	1.30.47.0	99.74	M. Hobson/ S. Collins (Yamaha)	22.15.0	101.74
			2 R. Biland/ K. Williams	Yamaha	1.31.46.8	98.66			
			3 R. Steinhausen/ W. Kalauch	Konig	1.31.50.0	98.60			
1978	**Senior 500cc**	226.38	1 T. Herron	Suzuki	2.1.33	111.74	P. Hennen	19.53.2	113.84 (Record)
			2 W. Guthrie	Suzuki	2.6.05				
			3 L. Mortimer	Yamaha	2.6.48				
	Junior 250cc	188.65	1 C. Mortimer	Yamaha	1.52.28	100.63	C. Mortimer	22.10.8	102.07
			2 C. Williams	Yamaha	1.52.57				
			3 T. Herron	Yamaha	1.53.56				
	Classic	226.38	1 M. Grant	Kawasaki	2.0.50	112.41	M. Grant	19.48	114.33 (Record)
			2 J. Williams	Suzuki	2.1.41				
			3 A. George	Yamaha	2.4.10				
	Formula One	226.38	1 M. Hailwood	Ducati	2.5.10	108.51	M. Hailwood	20.27	110.63 (Record)
			2 J. Williams	Honda					
			3 A. George	Yamaha					
	Sidecar Part I	113.19	1 R. Greaseley/ G. Russel	Busch-Yamaha	1.6.44	101.75	R. Biland/ K. Williams	21.48	103.81
			2 J. Taylor K. Arthur	Windle-Yamaha	1.7.05				
			3 G. Milton/ J. Brushwood	British Magnum	1.7.53				
	Sidecar Part II	113.19	1 R. Steinhausen/ W. Kalauch	Seymaz-Yamaha	1.12.30	93.67	R. Steinhausen/ W. Kalauch	23.32	96.14
			2 M. Boddice/ C. Birks	Woodhouse-Yamaha	1.14.13				
			3 J. Taylor/ K. Arthur	Windle-Yamaha	1.14.38				
1979	**Senior 500cc**	226.38	1 M. Hailwood	Suzuki	2.01.32	111.75	M. Hailwood	19.51.2	114.02 (Record)
			2 T. Rutter	Suzuki	2.03.39				
			3 D. Ireland	Suzuki	2.04.07				
	Junior 250cc	226.38	1 C. Williams	Yamaha	2.9.11	105.13	C. Williams	21.11.4	106.83 (Record)
			2 G. McGregor	Yamaha	2.10.19				
			3 I. Richards	Yamaha	2.10.25				
	Classic	226.38	1 A. George	Honda	2.00.07	113.92	A. George	19.49.6	114.18
			2 M. Hailwood	Suzuki	2.00.10				
			3 C. Williams	Yamaha	2.03.29				
	Formula One	226.38	1 A. George	Honda	2.02.50	110.57	A. George	20.02.6	112.94
			2 C. Williams	Honda	2.03.46				
			3 R. Haslam	Honda	2.05.00				
	Sidecar Part I	113.19	1 T. Ireson/ C. Pollington	Yamaha	1.06.29	102.14	Boddice/ Birks	21.55.4	103.26
			2 D. Greaseley/ J. Parkins	Yamaha	1.06.51				
			3 M. Boddice/ C. Birks	Woodhouse Yamaha	1.07.56				
	Sidecar Part II	113.18	1 T. Ireson/ C. Pollington	Yamaha	1.07.22	100.79	Steinhausen/ Arthur	22.09.4	102.17
			2 N. Rollason/ D. Homer	Barton Phoenix					
			3 D. Saville/ H. N. Sanderson	Yamaha					

Year	RACE Class	Miles	Rider	Machine	Time h.m.s.	Speed mph	Fastest Lap	Time m.s.	Speed mph
1980	**Senior 500cc**	226.38	1 G. Crosby	Suzuki	2.03.52	109.65	S. Woods	20.19.6	111.37
			2 S. Cull	Suzuki	2.04.45				
			3 S. Ward	Suzuki	2.05.05				
	Junior 250cc	150.92	1 C. Williams	Yamaha	1.28.34	102.22	D. Robinson	21.39.4	104.53
			2 D. Robinson	Yamaha	1.28.46				
			3 S. Tonkin	Cotton	1.29.06				
	Classic 1300cc	226.38	1 J. Dunlop	Yamaha	2.00.29	112.72	J. Dunlop	19.38.8	115.22 (Record)
			2 M. Grant	Honda	2.00.50				
			3 R. Haslam	Honda	2.03.02				
	Formula One	226.38	1 M. Grant	Honda	2.08.59	105.29	S. McClements	21.10.8	106.88
			2 G. Crosby	Suzuki	2.09.10				
			3 S. McClements	Honda	2.09.12				
	Sidecar Part I	113.19	1 T. Ireson/ C. Pollington	Yamaha	1.09.12	98.13	J. Taylor	22.20.0	100.61
			2 J. Taylor/ B. Johansson	Fowler-Yamaha	1.09.18				
			3 D. Greasley J. Parkins	Yamaha	1.10.12				
	Sidecar Part II	113.19	1 J. Taylor/ B. Johannsson	Fowler-Yamaha	1.05.34	103.55	J. Taylor	20.40	106.08 (Record)
			2 T. Ireson/ C. Pollington	Yamaha	1.06.41				
			3 N. Rollason/ D. Homer	Barton	1.07.02				